# PRIMARY CONCERNS
## GENDER FACTORS IN CHOOSING PRIMARY SCHOOL TEACHING

Report funded by the
**Equal Opportunities Commission for Northern Ireland**

*John Johnston*
*Eamonn McKeown*
*Alex McEwen*

Graduate School of Education
The Queen's University of Belfast

i

**Equal Opportunities Commission
for Northern Ireland**
Chamber of Commerce House
22 Great Victoria Street
Belfast BT2 7BA

Telephone: 01232 242752
Fax: 01232 331047
Legal and Research Fax: 01232 239879
e-mail: info@eocni.org.ni
Web site: http://www.eocni.org.uk


**1998**


**ISBN 0 906646 67 7**

# Contents

The study, funded by the Equal Opportunities Commission for Northern Ireland, is a response to concern about decreasing numbers of male teachers in primary schools. Recent statistics from the Teacher Training Agency reveal that in England and Wales, in the period 1980/1 to 1993/4, the percentage of male primary teachers decreased from 22% to 17% while the percentage of females increased from 78% to 83%. Although statistics for this period are not available for Northern Ireland, there is evidence of a similar trend in that the percentage of males decreased from 24% in 1987 to under 20% in 1997.

## OBJECTIVES AND METHODOLOGY

The central aim of this study is to explore the factors which influence choice of primary teaching as a career and account for the imbalance in the numbers of men and women choosing to become primary teachers. Data in the study were generated using a questionnaire developed in the light of relevant research literature and focus group responses from 36 sixth-form students in three grammar schools discussing teaching as a career option. A total of 1036 lower and upper sixth ('A Level') students (542 girls and 478 boys) from a representative sample of twelve grammar schools across Northern Ireland completed the questionnaire. A further 334 students in initial primary teacher training courses at Stranmillis and St. Mary's Colleges completed the questionnaire, modified for the purpose on the basis of focus group discussions with trainees in both institutions.

## MAIN FINDINGS

**1.** In Northern Ireland, the decline in the numbers of males in the primary teaching workforce reflects the general trends in England and Wales. In four of the five Education and Library Boards in Northern Ireland, the percentage of males in the primary teaching workforce decreased between 1992 and 1997. In one Board (NEELB) the percentage of males increased in this period (Paragraphs 3 and 4).

**2.** Patterns of recruitment of males to primary teaching in Northern Ireland are inherently volatile. Recent trends show the proportion of males entering primary teacher training, while still low relative to the proportion of females, to be at the highest level since 1978 (Paragraphs 5 -7).

**3.** The quality of the intake to primary teacher training in Northern Ireland, as measured by total A-Level points, is not only significantly higher than it is in England and Wales, it also continues to rise steeply (Paragraph 9).

**4.** Factors which influence the choice of primary teaching as a career have not previously been the subject of research in Northern Ireland. There is little empirical evidence relating specifically to such factors in other countries in the existing literature. Moreover, gender-related considerations in the process of career choice decision-making generally and in relation to teaching as a career in particular, are found to have received scant attention in previous research studies (Paragraphs 29 and 30).

**5.** Career preferences reveal that teaching is a first choice of 15% and a second choice of 17% of sixth-formers. Thus, approximately one third of A-Level students are seriously considering teaching as a career option (i.e. as first or second career choice). Of those naming teaching as their first choice of career, 67% are female and 33% male. Of those naming teaching as their second choice of career, 56% are female and 44% are male (Paragraph 36). Teaching as a career is seriously considered by 42% of males and 46% of females. Of this 42% of males, there is a clear bias in favour of secondary teaching with more than half (53%) aspiring to working in a secondary school while only 22% are considering primary teaching. On the other hand, among the 46% of females there is a tendency towards favouring primary teaching in their career considerations (Paragraph 38).

**6.** At the sixth-form stage, respondents have reasonably clear career preferences and these preferences vary in terms of the clarity or certainty with which they are held. Males and females aspiring to enter the teaching profession are not any more certain about their career choice than males and females generally, although females declaring their intention to teach in a primary school are marginally the most certain of all the groups (Paragraph 40).

**7.** Sixth-form males and females intending to pursue a career in teaching (regardless of whether this is in the primary or secondary sector) are influenced by factors similar to those governing career choice generally. They concur on the following:

- the status of teaching is not high relative to some other professions, but at the same time it carries prestige (Paragraphs 53, 57)
- career opportunity does not figure highly in choosing teaching as a career (Paragraphs 17 - 19)
- teaching is an intellectually stimulating occupation (Paragraph 56)
- teaching performs a moral service to society (Paragraph 49)
- primary teaching is associated with females (Paragraphs 45 - 47, 49)
- primary school teachers are seen as positive role models in relation to their choice of primary teaching as a career (Paragraphs 52 - 53, 65).

Teacher trainees claim to have been influenced by similar factors and report that the opportunity to work with children has also been a primary factor in their career choice (Paragraphs 20 and 21).

**8.** Male and female sixth-formers considering primary teaching as a career differ in a number of important respects:

- males are more likely than females to see primary teaching as a well-paid job (Paragraph 55)
- males attach greater weight than do females to extrinsic factors in choosing primary teaching as a career (Paragraph 51)
- males attach weight to perceived extrinsic rewards when making decisions about a possible career, whereas females place a premium on the potential of a career for intrinsic rewards (Paragraph 53)
- males are more likely than females to experience negative reaction from peers about choosing primary teaching as a career (Paragraphs 58, 59).

Male primary teacher trainees similarly place significantly greater emphasis on extrinsic aspects of teaching as a career and significantly less emphasis on intrinsic aspects than do their female counterparts (Paragraph 19).

**9.** Sixth-formers, whether considering teaching or not, and teacher trainees report complex associations between gendering and primary teaching. While reluctant to suggest that 'teaching is a woman's job', both groups believe that teaching is a career particularly suited to females. Although both see women as 'better' primary school teachers than men by an overwhelming margin, they assert the value of a male teacher presence in primary schools (Paragraphs 26, 27, 43 - 47).

**10.** Male sixth-formers considering primary teaching as a career and male trainees have the following perceptions of primary teaching:

- a job in which their 'maleness' is necessary and of value (Paragraph 25)
- a job suited to females, but not exclusively a woman's job (Paragraphs 22, 25, 49)
- a career choice which might be seen by their peers as inappropriate for males (Paragraphs 58, 59).
- a job in which as males they may have to confront societal negativity about males working closely with young children (Paragraphs 58, 59)
- a job which is not well-paid relative to other occupations (Paragraphs 21 - 23, 48, 49, 55).

**11.** Male sixth-formers not choosing primary teaching are likely to have been influenced by:

- a preference for going to university and obtaining a subject-specific degree (Paragraph 35)
- sensitivity regarding societal interpretation of males working with young children (Paragraphs 48, 58, 59)
- sensitivity about choosing a career in what is seen as a female-oriented domain (Paragraphs 41, 42)
- concern about peer disparagement or disapproval (Paragraphs 58, 59)
- negativity among their teachers towards teaching as a career (Appendix 3).

**12.** There are no statistically significant differences between male and female sixth-formers with regard to perceptions of the financial rewards of teaching. Teaching is low-ranked among occupations in terms of salary by both males and females, regardless of whether or not they are planning to pursue teaching as a career. Similarly, male and female trainees do not consider teaching well paid relative to other occupations (Paragraphs 21 - 23, 55).

**13.** While there is prestige associated with teaching, it is not highly ranked relative to other occupations in terms of status. There are no statistically significant differences between male and female sixth-formers with regard to perceptions of the status of teaching as an occupation (Paragraph 57). The status associated with teaching is not a strongly influential factor in male and female trainees' decision to enter teacher training (Paragraphs 18 and 19).

**14.** Regardless of gender, sixth-formers, whether considering teaching or not, and teacher trainees do not significantly differ in their opinion of primary teaching in a number of important respects. They rate teaching highly in terms of its potential for job satisfaction and value to society but see it less positively, relative to other occupations, in terms of its status in society and its potential for providing a good salary. (Paragraphs 22 - 24, 48-49).

**15.** There is no evidence to support the received wisdom that males considering primary teaching are influenced by prospects for career advancement. Although focus group responses indicate awareness of potential promotion prospects for males in primary teaching, male trainees rank this lowest of twelve factors influencing their choice of teaching as a career (Paragraphs 17 - 19). Male sixth-formers planning to enter primary teacher training are neutral as regards promotion prospects in primary teaching as a factor in career choice. Furthermore, with regard to responses concerning prospects for career advancement, there is no statistically significant difference between the views of male sixth-formers who plan to enter primary teacher training and their female counterparts (Appendix 3).

**16.** Peer group pressure is implicated as a factor in males not choosing primary teaching as a career. A significant proportion of male respondents suggest that they are afraid of being laughed at by their friends if they choose primary teaching. Males considering secondary teaching and females generally do not anticipate such a reaction (Paragraphs 58 and 59).

**17.** There is considerable evidence from the focus group discussions of a perception among males that when men choose to work with young children, there is a possibility that they may be suspected of potential paedophiliac tendencies. Girls do not perceive that females working with young children are similarly liable to suspicion. The currency of child abuse as an issue in public awareness may play a role in discouraging males from aspiring to careers requiring extensive contact with young children (Paragraph 48).

**18.** Focus group respondents comment adversely on the quantity and quality of career advice generally in schools. In mixed schools, there is evidence that females are more likely than males to be encouraged to consider primary teaching as a career (Paragraphs 33 and 34).

**1.** When the proposed General Teaching Council in Northern Ireland is established, its remit should include responsibility for monitoring recruitment to primary teaching and for ensuring that numbers of male applicants of suitable quality are maximised. While in England and Wales much of the responsibility in these respects falls within the remit and work of the Teacher Training Agency, currently in Northern Ireland there is no corresponding body (Main Findings 1, 2).

**2.** The Northern Ireland Teacher Education Committee and the Training and Employment Agency in Northern Ireland should include in their literature, information on teaching as a career and materials which articulate the particular contribution that men can make to teaching in the primary school (Main Findings 9, 10).

**3.** The impression gained by many young men, that in working with primary school age children they are somehow 'suspect', needs to be counteracted by literature promoting positive and 'safe' images of men working with young children. Careers conventions are an important outlet for the dissemination of such materials and perspectives (Main Finding 17).

**4.** Education and Library Boards, the Council for Catholic Maintained Schools and School Boards of Governors should review their policies and staff development training with respect to careers advice (Main Finding 18).

**5.** The quantity and quality of career information in schools about primary teaching should be improved and the career advice process more effectively matched to the needs of both males and females at the crucial stage of their career decision-making. Accordingly, a briefing document which outlines the main findings of this research, showing the views of sixth-formers on teaching as a career, on career advice and the factors found to be influential in career decision-making, should be made available to all careers teachers in schools (Main Findings 5, 7 - 18).

**6.** Gender-stereotyping in relation to occupations such as teaching should be challenged during careers advice seminars. Careers teachers should be encouraged to include young male teachers in their career briefing programmes in order to counteract males' experience of negative views of teaching among their contemporaries. Additionally, teachers generally should be encouraged to be even-handed in their modelling of teaching as an occupation (Main Findings 7, 10, 16).

**7.** Universities and Colleges should be proactive during open days and visits to schools in promoting primary teaching as a valid and valuable male career. In promoting and publicising their courses, more extensive use should be made of literature and other appropriate audio-visual materials showing positive images of male teacher presence in primary classrooms (Main Findings 10, 11).

**8.** Whilst ensuring that teaching appointments are based on merit, the Department of Education for Northern Ireland, the Council for Catholic Maintained Schools, the Education and Library Boards and primary school Boards of Governors should monitor the gender balance of teachers in schools (Main Finding 1).

**9.** The high quality of intake to teacher training in Northern Ireland indicates both the high regard in which education is held in Northern Ireland and the extent to which numbers are 'capped'. In seeking equity of treatment, the Department of Education for Northern Ireland should monitor closely the abilities of those who complete training outside and subsequently return to Northern Ireland seeking teaching appointments (Main Finding 3).

FURTHER RESEARCH

**1.** Further research is required to investigate how the quantity and quality of career information can be maximised and how career advice can be best matched to the needs of both males and females at the crucial stage of their career decision-making.

**2.** The extent to which fear of suspicion relating to males working with young children acts as a dissuading factor among males in career decision-making with regard to primary teaching should be specifically researched.

# Section 1

## INTRODUCTION

### *Focus of the study*

1. Funded by the Equal Opportunities Commission for Northern Ireland, this study focused on recruitment to teaching in the primary sector. The central aim of the study, the first on the subject in Northern Ireland, was to investigate factors which influence whether or not primary teaching is chosen as a career and the role gender plays among sixth-formers and teacher-trainees in this decision-making process. Gender issues have received little attention in studies in the area of career choice in general and in studies of primary teaching in particular. The objective was to generate data from a wide range of perspectives, to permit clarification of: (a) trends in the recruitment of male primary school teachers; (b) factors influencing primary teaching as a career choice; (c) the underlying equal opportunities issues; and (d) the policy implications, if any, for the work of the Equal Opportunities Commission in Northern Ireland and policy makers in all agencies responsible for education in Northern Ireland.

### *Background to the study*

2. This study is set in the context of current concern regarding issues of quality and quantity in the recruitment of teachers in Britain. Recent statistics for England and Wales reveal a significant increase in the imbalance in numbers of males and females in primary school teaching. In the period 1980 to 1994 the percentage of males decreased from 22% to 17% while the percentage of females increased from 78% to 83%. Anthea Millet, Chief Executive of the Teacher Training Agency, has recently speculated that on recent trends, male teachers could disappear from primary schools by the year 2010. There is a growing concern among educationalists that as a consequence, a proper balance of male and female adult roles in their differing approaches to children's learning may not be maintained in the educational experience of younger children.

## Section 2

**3.** There has been a decrease in the percentage of males in the primary teaching force in Northern Ireland from 24% in 1987 to 20% in 1997. This suggests that the trends which are the focus of concern in England and Wales exist also in Northern Ireland. However, when this 4% decrease is examined more carefully it becomes clear that caution is required in its interpretation, since there is evidence that it is not uniform. The statistics for the percentage of males in the teaching force in each of Northern Ireland's five Education and Library Boards' primary schools over the period of the last five years indicate that there are inter-Board variations underlying this general decrease (Figure 1). While in four of the five Boards the percentage of males decreased between 1992 and 1997, in one Board (NEELB) the percentage of males actually increased in this period.

Figure 1 – Males as a percentage of the teaching force in Primary Schools
*(by Education & Library Board)*

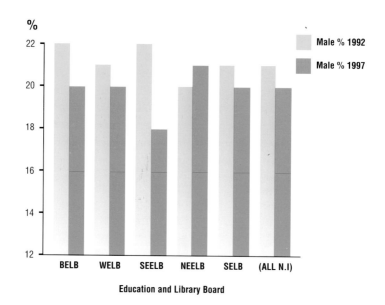

**4.** In Northern Ireland, the overall percentage of males in the primary teaching force in 1997 (20%) masks a substantial difference between the percentages of male primary teachers in the Controlled and Catholic Maintained sectors (16% and 23% respectively), and variations across Education and Library Boards. Illumination of these differences is provided when changes in the percentage of the primary school teaching force accounted for by males is analysed by school management type (Figures 2 and 3). In both the Belfast (BELB) and South-Eastern (SEELB) Boards, the decreasing percentage of males occurs in both types of schools, although the size of the decrease from 1992 to 1997 is substantially greater in the latter (from 20% to 16% in Controlled schools and from 28% to 20% in Catholic Maintained Schools). In addition to these between-Board differences, there are within-Board differences. In Western Education and Library Board (WELB), while the percentage of male teachers in Controlled Schools fell from 15% to 13% between 1992 and 1997, the corresponding figures for Catholic Maintained Schools show that the percentage of male primary teachers has not altered in the period. In North-Eastern Board (NEELB) on the other hand, the percentage of male teachers in Controlled Schools has remained constant between 1992 and 1997, whereas the corresponding figures for Catholic Maintained schools in that Board show an increase over the period from 23% to 25%.

**Figure 2 – Males as a percentage of the teaching force in Controlled Primary Schools**
   *(by Education & Library Board)*

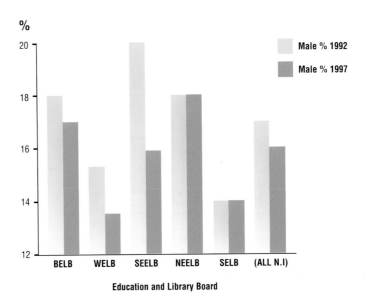

**Education and Library Board**

Figure 3 - Males as a percentage of the teaching force in Catholic Maintained Primary Schools *(by Education & Library Board)*

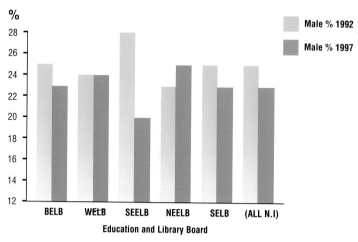

## Recruitment of males into primary teaching

5. Further insight on gender patterns in the primary teaching force in Northern Ireland is afforded by figures for the recruitment of males to primary teaching. Statistics for entry to the Initial Teacher Training BEd (Primary) course in St Mary's and Stranmillis Colleges show that, despite there having been variations in the total numbers of entrants, the proportion of males to females has remained small (Figure 4).

Figure 4 - Entrants to BEd (Primary ): 1978 - 1996

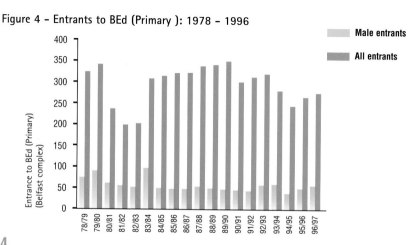

Figure 5 - Male entrants to BEd (Primary) as a percentage of total intake: 1978 - 96

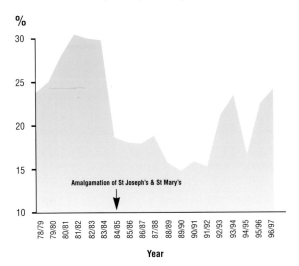

**6.** Moreover, although the most recent statistical evidence is of an increasing percentage of males in the intake to the primary BEd course in these Colleges (Figure 5), the pattern over the last twenty years is one of considerable volatility. The percentage of the total intake accounted for by males has fluctuated significantly, from a high of over 30% in the early to mid-1980's to a low of under 15 % in 1989/90. By 1996/97, after a period of instability, the percentage of males in the total BEd (Primary) intake had risen to 23%, its highest level since 1983/4, when the closure of St Joseph's College, catering only for male teacher trainees, was perhaps a factor in the recruitment of male trainees. At face value this most recent trend is a healthy one and, were it to continue into the future, would mean that the recruitment of males to primary teaching in Northern Ireland, while not justifying complacency, would be less concerning than are current predictions for recruitment in England and Wales.

**7.** However, the degree of volatility evident in the pattern shown in Figure 5 sounds an important note of caution and this is emphasised by analysis of the percentage of males in the intake figures for BEd (Primary) by College. As is shown in Figure 6, the relatively high percentage of males in the intake to BEd (Primary) in 1996/97 is largely accounted for by an unusually high percentage of males in the 1996/97 intake to St Mary's College, and by a corresponding decrease in the intake of males to BEd (Primary) in Stranmillis College. Taken together the evidence above points to the need for care in interpreting the figures for males as a percentage of the primary teaching force in Northern Ireland. Despite appearing at face value to be a healthy and improving situation and one which is quite different from that which is fuelling concern in England and Wales, the degree of volatility and underlying variability is concerning and requires not only continued monitoring but elaboration as to its causation.

Figure 6 - Male entrants to BEd (Primary) as a percentage of total intake:
*1978 - 96 (by College)*

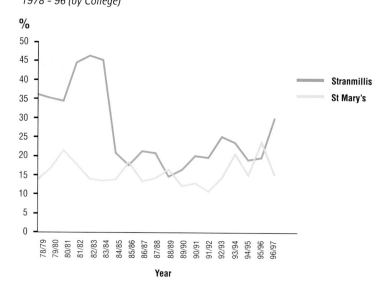

## Application for entry to training for primary teaching

**8.** The concern in England and Wales with regard to the recruitment of males to primary teaching is compounded by a general decline in the numbers of males and females applying for entry to initial training courses. This decline is referred to in a comprehensive report published by the House of Commons Education and Employment Select Committee (HMSO, 1997). While the Report does not make specific reference to gender (and is thus consistent with much of the existing literature in this regard), it states:

> There are clear and disturbing signs that problems exist in respect of both the quantity and the quality of entrants to the profession, coupled with shortages of teachers in some areas of the country and in some subjects (Para 2).

According to evidence submitted to the Select Committee by the Teacher Training Agency for England and Wales, in 1996 primary courses attracted sufficient numbers of applicants: there were 2.19 applicants for each place on a primary undergraduate course and 2.56 applicants for each place on a primary post-graduate course. However, forecasts were for a drop of 11% in applications to undergraduate initial teacher training courses (most of which are for primary) in 1997.

**9.** In Northern Ireland, on the other hand, there is evidence that similar decreases in applications do not pertain. Not only are application rates for BEd courses increasing, but the quality of entrants as measured by total A-Level points continues to rise (Figure 7).

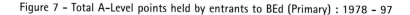

Figure 7 - Total A-Level points held by entrants to BEd (Primary) : 1978 - 97

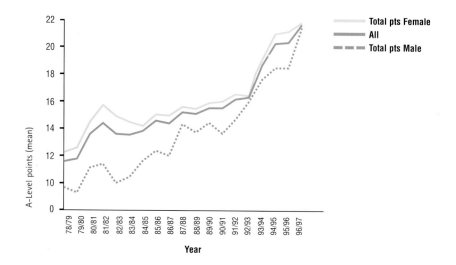

During the last twenty years the quality of entrant to undergraduate primary teacher training in Stranmillis and St Mary's Colleges has consistently increased. Whereas in 1996/97 (most recent figures available), in England and Wales the mean A-Level points total of entrants to undergraduate primary teacher training was 12.9 for males and 14.0 for females (DfEE, 1997), in Northern Ireland the comparable means for entry to Stranmillis and St Mary's Colleges are 21.3 for males and 21.5 for females. Arguably explanations for this include the fact that numbers entering teacher training are tightly 'capped' by the Department of Education for Northern Ireland. Together with a strong regionality in terms of the high regard in which education is widely held in Northern Ireland, this operates to ensure that competition for restricted places is strong. In any case, these figures draw attention not only to the very high quality of entrants to primary teacher training in Northern Ireland relative to entrants in England and Wales, but also to the fact that in Northern Ireland the long-standing disparity between male and female entrants has all but disappeared.

## Section 3

**10.** The evidence above suggests that recruitment of males to primary teaching in Northern Ireland is relatively healthy both in terms of quantity and quality. However, it remains the case that the vast majority of those considering primary teaching as a career are female and the factors at play in this phenomenon are inadequately understood. The present study sought to extend what is currently known about these variables and examine how they operate with regard to primary teaching as a career choice. In order to facilitate a comprehensive analysis of the issues under investigation, data were generated from a review of the literature dealing with teaching career choices, from open-ended focus group discussions and from the administration of questionnaires designed specifically for the study.

### Data generation: focus groups

**11.** A focus group concentrates on discussion of a particular topic or topics and typically consists of eight to twelve participants. The group is facilitated by one or more moderators who follow a relatively unstructured interview schedule. Focus groups can generate data which are not obtainable through paper and pencil self-report measures or observational measures and provide qualitative information which can illuminate underlying attitudes, opinions, and behaviour preferences. The advantages of the focus group approach to data generation lie in its potential for reduced inhibition on the part of participants, the generation of wide ranging responses, and the creation of a valuable source of exploratory information.

**12.** Eight focus group discussions were conducted in January and February 1997. These discussions involved a total of 33 sixth-form students (both male and female drawn from three high schools located in Belfast, County Antrim and County Tyrone), 10 BEd. students (from St. Mary's and Stranmillis Colleges), four MEd. students, three careers teachers, and two college admissions tutors (from St. Mary's and Stranmillis). The discussions, each lasting 45-60 minutes, were recorded and subsequently transcribed. In conducting the focus group discussions with A-Level students the objectives were to generate information as to the career aspirations of A-level students, the influences governing such aspirations, whether teaching as a career has been considered, perceptions of teaching as a career, and factors influencing the development of these perceptions (see Appendix 1). In discussions with the BEd. and MEd. groups (all males who have already made the decision to pursue a career in primary teaching), the focus was on ascertaining the reasons why they chose to enter primary teacher training.

## Data generation: questionnaire

**13.** The data generated from the discussions, together with material drawn from relevant literature, informed the construction of a questionnaire appropriate to sixth-form respondents (Appendix 2 Part 1). The questionnaire elicited perceptions with regard to careers and career choice, before asking detailed questions concerning respondents' attitudes towards teaching. The first section included questions dealing with factors that might be important when choosing a career, respondents' career ambitions and whether or not they view their chosen career as dominated by one or other gender. The second section dealt specifically with perceptions of teaching. Pilot testing of the questionnaire with a sixth-form cohort (n= 96) was carried out. After minor alterations to the wording of three questions, it was administered to a total of 1036 sixth-form students at eight schools in March 1997. The school sample was made up of boys-only, girls-only and mixed-sex institutions. These schools, from both the Controlled and Catholic Maintained sectors, were located in both rural and urban settings. The sample comprised 558 females (54%) and 478 males (46%), of whom 57% were in lower sixth-form and 43% in upper sixth-form. Approximately 98% of respondents were taking three subjects at A-Level, with the remainder studying either two or four subjects.

**14.** The questionnaire was adapted for administration to students currently undergoing teacher training (Appendix 2 Part 2) and this version was administered to a structured opportunity sample of 334 first, second and third year BEd students in St. Mary's and Stranmillis Colleges. Of these, 15% were male and 85% were female.

**Section 4**

# CHOOSING PRIMARY TEACHING AS A CAREER -
# THE VIEWS OF THOSE IN TRAINING

### Trainee perceptions of primary teaching

**15.** While the issues relating to why teacher trainees in Northern Ireland have decided to teach have not been documented, the topic has been addressed in other countries (e.g. Thomas, 1984; Ethington, 1988; Evans, 1993). Studies reported in the literature indicate that decision-making in choosing teaching as an occupation is likely to involve an interplay among social, economic, circumstantial and individual factors. While individual interests and aptitudes play an important role, the perceived attractiveness of the work of teaching is also influential. Specific requirements and circumstances that might hinder or facilitate entry to the teaching profession at a particular time, and access to information about teaching as an occupation, are also shown to be important considerations.

**16.** A number of previous studies have addressed the factors influencing choice of teaching as a career. However the issue of gender as a factor has generally been ignored. In the United States, Thomas (1984) found that the factors most influencing teaching as a career choice were altruistic and included the desire to work with children and the desire to impart knowledge. Again in the United States, Lortie (1975) found that the attractiveness of teaching as a career relates to the opportunities it affords in terms of working with young people, performing a moral service to society, working in a school setting, job security and agreeable hours and holidays. Ethington (1988) confirmed Lortie's findings, reporting that 97% of his sample saw working with children as the major reason why teaching was selected as a career. Evans (1993) in her study of factors influencing teaching as a career in Jamaica, concentrated on students who had already made the decision to teach. Her findings were that prospective teachers are attracted by the idea of service, of working with children, and in many cases have been influenced by family members and their own (positive) educational experiences.

**17.** The present study sought to explicate the factors which might have informed the decision to pursue teaching as a career by a sample of primary teacher trainees in Northern Ireland. Below is a sample of comments in focus group discussion with male trainees regarding possible factors:

> Most of my experience is with younger children. I get on very well with them.

> I had quite a bit of experience working with children outside school and I felt I could get quite a good laugh; I knew it was something I would enjoy doing and that was what I felt was most important.

> I know that I will definitely get a job when I finish College because there are so few men in primary school teaching. I was told that as a man you will just walk into a job.

> At least we are guaranteed a job. You start off on whatever salary it is and you just work your way up. There is the promise of a certain amount of security because there are always going to be children to teach.

> My father advised me to go into education. He said that I could be a headmaster in a few years. He said that there was a lot more opportunity for promotion in a primary school so he encouraged that.

**18.** The questionnaire subsequently presented the primary trainee-teacher respondents (n=334) with a list of twelve factors shown to be relevant, both by focus group discussion responses such as the above and by a review of pertinent studies. These were: working with children; perceived job satisfaction; contribution to society; imparting knowledge; job security; salary; mentally stimulating work; good holidays; respectable job; family approval; status; and, promotion prospects. Respondents were asked to rank the factors in order of importance where 1 = most important and 12 = least important.

## Table 1: Perception of Primary Teaching – Rank order by gender[1]
### (Teacher Trainees)

| Factor | All Males (n=50) | | | All Females (n=284) | | | Sig. |
|---|---|---|---|---|---|---|---|
| | Rank | Mean | SD | Rank | Mean | SD | |
| Working with children | 1 | 3.022 | 1.960 | 1 | 2.357 | 2.239 | * |
| Perceived job satisfaction | 2 | 3.574 | 2.811 | 2 | 3.178 | 2.316 | ns |
| Contribution to society | 3 | 5.429 | 3.343 | 3 | 5.064 | 2.804 | ns |
| Imparting knowledge | 4 | 5.767 | 3.344 | 4 | 5.081 | 2.925 | ns |
| Job security | 5 | 5.795 | 3.460 | 7 | 6.528 | 3.155 | ns |
| Salary | 6 | 6.068 | 3.216 | 9 | 7.086 | 2.805 | *** |
| Mentally stimulating work | 7 | 6.488 | 3.090 | 5 | 5.824 | 2.941 | ns |
| Good holidays | 8 | 6.556 | 3.108 | 8 | 6.782 | 3.026 | ns |
| Respectable job | 9 | 6.905 | 2.712 | 6 | 6.455 | 2.668 | ns |
| Family approval | 10 | 8.756 | 3.277 | 10 | 9.084 | 2.805 | ns |
| Status | 11 | 8. 854 | 2.555 | 11 | 9.131 | 2.327 | ns |
| Promotion prospects | 12 | 9.050 | 1.999 | 12 | 9.137 | 2.579 | ns |

* = p<.05; *** = p<.001; ns = p>.05

[1] Significance tests are aimed at revealing whether or not the difference between two means could be ascribed to chance factors operating at the time the sample was selected. If the difference can not be explained as being due solely to chance, the difference between the theory and the sample result is said to be statistically significant. Significance is measured at different levels: a significance level of 5% (p<.05) indicates that there are only five chances in a hundred that the observed difference can be explained by chance. When the level is shown to be p<.001, this is reduced to one chance in a thousand, and the difference between means is therefore referred to as highly significant. For example, in Table 1 the difference between the two means relating to 'salary' is found to be highly significant (p<.001), which means that the different weight which males and females attach to this aspect of teaching is particularly noteworthy since the likelihood that the difference has arisen by chance is a negligible one. SD in Table 1 and in subsequent Tables refers to standard deviation, an index of the spread or dispersion of sample responses.

**19.** In ranking these factors (Table 1), male and female trainees concur on the four most influential factors in choosing to become a primary teacher and these relate to altruistic aspects of being a teacher. There are no significant between-group differences in means across the various factors except in relation to the importance of working with children ($p<.05$) and the importance of salary as a factor influencing choice. This indicates that in deciding to become a primary teacher, males place significantly less emphasis than females on the importance of working with children. It is worthy of note that, although differences between means are not always statistically significantly different[2], females place greater weight on intrinsic aspects whereas males are more influenced by extrinsic aspects of teaching as a career[3]. With regard to salary as a factor (ranked sixth by males and ninth by females), there is a highly significant difference between the corresponding means ($p<.001$).

### *Trainee perceptions of teaching as an occupation*

**20.** Teacher trainees have chosen teaching as a career from a wide range of career alternatives. They have done so as the result of a process of reflection involving many factors. The Report of the House of Commons Education and Employment Select Committee (HMSO, 1997) recognised the competition from other potential career paths:

> Many other professions have a more attractive image than teaching; pay is felt to be better in many other jobs and employers in other fields generally pay for their employees' training; and the working conditions are also seen as better in other walks of life. .... It should be borne in mind that competition from other professions may be based to some extent on people's perceptions of different jobs, rather than the actuality (Paras 42 - 43).

---

[2] *It may appear anomalous that while both males and females give the same ranking to 'working with children' there is a significant difference between the means. This can be explained by the fact that although both groups give the highest priority to this aspect of teaching, the strength with which females assert the primacy of working with children is substantively greater than it is for males. This explains the statistically significant difference reported in Table 1.*

[3] *There are numerous references in this report to intrinsic and extrinsic aspects of teaching as a career. Intrinsic aspects are those which are inherent in the actual performance of the job (e.g. working with children). Extrinsic aspects are those relating to the external context in which the job is performed (e.g. how well teachers are remunerated, the status associated with teaching).*

**21.** Consequently, in order to examine Northern Ireland trainees' perceptions of teaching as an occupation relative to other occupations which might be considered in choosing a career, respondents were presented with a list of ten jobs which they were asked to rank according to a number of factors. The ten were: Computer Programmer; Lawyer; Engineer; Journalist; Accountant; Doctor; Politician; Teacher; Electrician and Nurse. Respondents were asked to select and rank-order the three careers which they felt were of most value to society, have the greatest potential for job satisfaction, have highest status in the local community, require good communication skills, are most suited to females and males, and which offer the greatest potential for a 'good' salary. A specific interest of the study was to examine responses for the existence of gender differences. This was found not to have been a specific focus in previous studies in the area.

**Table 2: Perception of Careers – Rank order by gender**
  *(Teacher Trainees)*

| Occupation | Value to society | | Potential for job satisfaction | | Status in the local community | | Requiring personal comm. skills | | Most suited to females | | Potential for good salary | | Most suited to males | |
|---|---|---|---|---|---|---|---|---|---|---|---|---|---|---|
| | M | F | M | F | M | F | M | F | M | F | M | F | M | F |
| Comp. Prog. | 9 | 9 | 9 | 9 | 7 | 7 | 10 | 10 | 8 | 8 | 5 | 5 | 5 | 3 |
| Lawyer | 6 | 4 | 4 | 4 | 2 | 1 | 2 | 5 | 5 | 5 | 1 | 1 | 3 | 7 |
| Engineer | 8 | 6 | 7 | 7 | 9 | 8 | 9 | 9 | 9 | 9 | 6 | 6 | 1 | 1 |
| Journalist | 5 | 8 | 5 | 5 | 8 | 4 | 4 | 3 | 3 | 3 | 7 | 7 | 8 | 8 |
| Accountant | 10 | 10 | 10 | 10 | 4 | 6 | 7 | 7 | 6 | 6 | 3 | 3 | 4 | 5 |
| Doctor | 1 | 2 | 2 | 2 | 1 | 2 | 5 | 2 | 4 | 4 | 2 | 2 | 6 | 6 |
| Politician | 4 | 5 | 8 | 7 | 3 | 3 | 3 | 6 | 7 | 7 | 4 | 4 | 7 | 4 |
| Teacher | 2 | 1 | 1 | 1 | 5 | 5 | 1 | 1 | 1 | 1 | 8 | 8 | 9 | 9 |
| Electrician | 7 | 8 | 7 | 8 | 10 | 10 | 8 | 8 | 10 | 10 | 9 | 9 | 2 | 2 |
| Nurse | 3 | 3 | 3 | 3 | 6 | 9 | 6 | 4 | 2 | 2 | 10 | 10 | 10 | 10 |

**22.** From the summary of responses presented in Table 2 it is clear that, as is perhaps predictable, teaching as an occupation is generally highly regarded by trainees relative to the other occupations listed. This is broadly consistent with the findings of research conducted for the Teacher Training Agency in England and Wales (Hill and Knowlton, 1995) on the general public's image of teaching. In that study, teaching was similarly highly ranked in terms of its value to society, its potential for job satisfaction, and as an occupation requiring communication skills.

**23.** The rankings of the occupation of teacher by male and female trainees in the present study are almost identical across the six variables (Table 2). Both see teaching as the occupation which most requires communication skills, which has the greatest potential for job satisfaction, and which is most suited to women. Female respondents regard teaching as the occupation in this list which is of most value to society, whereas males rank it second behind doctor. Teaching is not so positively viewed relative to the other occupations listed when it comes to status and salary.

**24.** In the questionnaire, teacher trainees were presented with a list of statements relating to teaching and were asked for attitudinal responses on a five point scale ranging from 'strongly agree' to 'strongly disagree' (See Appendix 4 for a detailed summary of the responses). The high ranking of teaching with regard to 'value to society' shown in Table 2 is corroborated by trainees' responses to the attitudinal statement: 'teachers perform a moral service to society' in the questionnaire. Only two respondents out of a total of 334 disagreed with the statement, and there was no statistically significant difference ($p>.05$) between the responses of males and females. The ranking of teaching as first in the list of occupations in terms of 'potential for job-satisfaction' is illuminated by responses which strongly agree, irrespective of gender, with the statement: 'teaching is an intellectually stimulating occupation'. While trainees' perception of the status of teaching is not particularly high relative to the status of other occupations, both males and females generally agree that the 'community looks up to teachers'. The ranking of teaching as eighth in the list of occupations is consistent with the general disagreement of respondents, regardless of gender, with the statement: 'teaching is a well-paid job'.

**25.** The ranking of teaching as the occupation in the list which is close to being 'least suited to males' and which is 'most suited to females' is of relevance to the focus of this study. The evidence is that there are many aspects inherent in these perceptions and the complexity is only revealed by examination of the responses to the relevant attitudinal statements. Firstly, male trainees' choice of primary teaching as a career involves their association of teaching with females, reflected in their ranking of teaching as first among the occupations most 'suited to females'. Even though they are male, are themselves to become primary teachers and the teacher gender in the statement was not specified, there was general agreement among male trainees with the statement 'in primary school, the role of a teacher is an extension of that of a mother'. This is reflected in the views expressed in focus group discussions, typified by the following response:

> I suppose it is a fact that it is best for a woman to look after children in P1; I know that I couldn't teach P1. I taught P2 last year and found it very difficult. Maybe those age groups are more for women.

This indicates an internalisation of 'femaleness' with regard to primary teaching. As one male trainee acknowledged during focus group discussion:

> I think that there is a danger that the woman is getting stereotyped into the primary school role. That is having a knock-on effect for people going to teaching. It is not instilled in the man's mind; he has grown up with it all these years.

This suggests a low association by them between teaching and males. However responses to the statements 'teaching is a woman's job' and 'it is inappropriate for males to teach very young children' strongly suggest that this low association does not translate into notions of inappropriateness. Moreover, males believe it is important that males teach in primary schools and value the contribution that teaching by males can make:

> I think it is important to have a male teacher .... like with your parents you need both a male and a female to guide you and so in your education you need some experience of both to learn .... you do learn from your teachers (Male trainee during focus group discussion).

> Most primary school teachers are female as far as I can see. If you don't have a male teacher in primary school, then secondary school is going to be even more of a shock. I was taught by a man in Primary 5 and Primary 7. I think that this was important. (Male trainee during focus group discussion).

Furthermore, male trainees' strong agreement with the statements, 'if there were no male teachers in primary schools, children would be disadvantaged' and 'all primary school children should be taught by a man for at least one year', is indicative of something akin to a moral stance. The corresponding responses of female trainees place significantly less value (p<.001) on the contribution of a male presence in primary teaching.

Associated with these perceptions regarding the gendering of primary teaching is the expectation among male trainees that those who choose primary teaching may experience negative reaction from their peers:

> Most people at school went into engineering and the like ... the male courses. Whereas if you go into teaching it is seen as more of a female course and you can expect some stick from your friends. (Male trainee during focus group discussion).

> There are always disparaging comments that you are doing a Mickey Mouse woman's course .... your friends at Christmas will make jokes and ask how you are getting on with the wee kiddies. To an extent it is only joking, but they do look down. (Male trainee during focus group discussion).

**26.** To further investigate the extent to which trainees' views of teaching are associated with gender, respondents were asked three questions relating to whether or not they differentiate between males and females with regard to which make the 'better' teachers.

**Table 3: Perceptions of who makes 'better' teachers**
   *(Teacher Trainees)*

| Respondent | Who makes the 'better' Primary Teacher? | | Who makes the 'better' Secondary Teacher? | |
|---|---|---|---|---|
| | M | F | M | F |
| | (n=50) | (n=284) | (n=50) | (n=284) |
| Males are 'better' than females | 2% | 1% | 40% | 9% |
| Females are 'better' than males | 28% | 42% | 0% | 2% |
| No difference | 60% | 52% | 52% | 83% |
| No opinion | 10% | 5% | 8% | 5% |

**27.** While the majority of both male and female trainees do not differentiate between males and females as the 'better' teachers, the most salient aspect of the findings presented in Table 3 is the clear disposition among all trainees regardless of gender, towards females as the 'better' primary teachers. This is not sustained in their perception of secondary teachers. The 28% of male trainees who see females as 'better' in the career they themselves intend to pursue is a substantial proportion of that cohort and further illustrates the view among all respondents that females are somehow more able and effective than males as teachers in a primary school setting. However, males regard their own gender more highly when it comes to secondary teaching, with 40% suggesting that men make 'better' secondary teachers than do women. In contrast, while 42% of females differentiate in favour of their own gender more highly in relation to primary teaching, this is not the case with regard to secondary teaching. Indeed, the generally high rating for females as primary school teachers contrasts with the negligible percentages of the respective samples regarding women as 'better' teachers at secondary level.

**28.** These results indicate that trainees hold perceptions of teaching which are differentiated by whether the context is the primary or the secondary setting. The general male bias towards females and against males as the 'better' primary school teachers suggests that males associate women and primary teaching. Insofar as this is the case, it may well have resonances which become expressed in the relatively smaller numbers of males entering primary teacher training (see Figure 4).

## Section 5

29. The making of career choices generally, and in relation to teaching in particular, is a complex process and one about which not enough is known. No empirical evidence relating specifically to primary teaching as a career choice was uncovered by a search for literature relevant to the present study. Rather the focus of previous research has been on teaching generally. Studies of teaching as a career have concentrated on high school and other second level students who have already made the decision to be teachers. Such studies typically have investigated factors perceived to have influenced the decision to follow the path chosen. This study seeks to contribute to what is known about variables which influence whether or not teaching is a career choice. It also seeks to extend what is known by investigating why primary teaching as a career may not be the choice of male school leavers and whether gender issues influence such decisions.

30. Ginzberg's seminal study (Ginzberg 1951), although not gender-specific, identified key variables involved in the career decision-making process in general and demonstrated how such decisions constitute a developmental process which takes place over a number of years. He outlined three phases of development in choosing a career: the fantasy period, usually from early childhood to the age of 11; the tentative period, from age 11 to near the end of high school; and the realistic period, from age 17 onwards. Respondents in the present study fall into the last of these categories. With reference to Ginzberg's model, Holland (1973) found that people in this realistic stage of decision-making select occupations through which they can express their personalities and which will provide them with experiences appropriate to their personalities. Similarly, Super *et al* (1963) showed that such individuals choose occupations with characteristics which they perceive will allow them to function in a role that is consistent with their environmental history.

31. Teaching as a career is perhaps unique in that all individuals become aware of teaching by virtue of their compulsory attendance at school. Thus high school students are likely to have first hand knowledge of what teaching entails and internalised notions about its merits and drawbacks as a potential career choice. For example, Hutchinson and Johnston (1994) found that high school students in California who were committed to pursuing teaching claimed to have been influenced in their views of teaching as a career by their own experiences of being taught. This work, however, focused only on high school students who wanted to be teachers and data were not collected on the factors operating to discourage their peers from pursuing teaching. Indeed, it is the case that in such previous research, scant attention has been given to those who have decided not to teach and the factors that might have dissuaded them from pursuing a career in teaching.

32. Furthermore, there is a paucity of empirical evidence as to the role played by gender in the making of choices about teaching as a career. An exception to this is a recent research study in the United States (Newby *et al*, 1995) which investigated African-American high school students' perceptions of teaching as a career and the influence upon these perceptions of selected social background characteristics. Part of Newby's study involved investigation of the influence of gender on receptivity to teaching as a career. The findings were that females evaluate the importance of teaching more highly than do males. Also, males who did choose teaching were more likely than females to have been influenced by others in making this career choice.

## Careers advice

33. Focus group discussion with college admissions tutors, in which they reflected on their experience of interviewing applicants for entry to primary teacher training courses, raised a number of interesting perspectives on careers advice in schools:

> There are some schools, particularly grammar schools, and we are recruiting mostly from the grammar schools, where there would seem to be a rank order of the professions based on their greatest publicity value for the school. Some professions are seen as carrying more points and teaching would, until recently at any rate, have been low in that pecking order.

> There are definitely schools where the careers teacher, if he or she thought the pupil was going to get As and Bs and they mentioned teaching, then the pupil would be encouraged to look at something else. There seems to be a 'You can do better than that' sort of attitude. I am not sure if that is a trend but it is something that I would find in particular schools.

Some careers teachers are awfully misguided and are not keeping up with the requirements.

There are some applicants who are extremely well prepared and there are those for whom the preparation has been totally inadequate. I think I would put a lot of blame on careers teachers in schools. We thought that we would do something to redress this and to give everybody an equal opportunity. Three years ago I issued quite detailed documentation for careers teachers and also for candidates who were applying and being short listed for interviews, guiding them on the kind of issues that would be raised at the interview. Some interviewees couldn't even recall having received the documentation.

Males interviewees might not be as well prepared as female interviewees and generally are less confident. They would be more timorous than females in communicating qualities such as enthusiasm and motivation and so on. The men would be a little harder to draw out in terms of expressing their motivation for teaching. I don't know if it is something to do with the male psyche or whether it is that they are a bit more cool about the whole thing. They do require a little more persuading and coaxing.

I have found that a lot of applicants refer to work experience as something that engendered, stimulated or confirmed their interest in primary teaching. I also think that there can be a strong family influence where teaching is already somewhere within the family. Those who don't have teachers in the family, would sometimes talk about a particular teacher who has had an influence on them.

Up until recently, publicity materials were probably quite girl-oriented. They depicted groups of mainly female student teachers working with groups of children. There tended to be more females than males in the pictures in the prospectus. In the last year or two we have been working quite hard getting together photographs and pictures of male teachers working with mixed groups of children.

We haven't got to the stage of going out to schools, knocking their doors and saying 'I want to give your boys a talk'. If I did have time I would like to go to schools and demystify some of the elements of teaching as a career for men, but there is no time to do that.

**34.** These views illuminate several issues relating to both the quantity and quality of career advice in schools and are corroborated by evidence from the focus group responses of teacher trainees. Trainees report that careers advice in schools regarding primary teaching as a career is of variable quality and that females are more actively encouraged than males to consider primary teaching as a career. For example one male trainee said:

I was not actively encouraged to pursue my interest in primary teaching. In no way do I want to be sexist, but to me the people who were actively encouraged were the girls, especially those who were expected to get 2 A's and a B or 3 A's. To me they were actively encouraged to go for it. I can say that I was the only male from my Grammar School who went for an interview at Stranmillis that year.

Given that careers advice is usually most prominent at the sixth-form stage, the evidence above clearly suggests that the quality and quantity of careers advice in schools can be implicated as a factor in whether or not males consider primary teaching as a career.

### *Teaching as a career consideration among A-Level students*

**35.** In the present study, sixth-form students were surveyed as to their immediate post A-Level plans. The findings are that an overwhelming majority (95% of females and 93% of males) aspire to third level education upon the completion of their A-Level course (Table 4).[4]

Table 4: Post A-Level Aspiration (A-Level students)

| Plan | All (n=1036) | Males (n=479) | Females (n=557) |
|---|---|---|---|
| Go to university | 88% | 89% | 87% |
| Go to teacher training college | 6% | 4% | 8% |
| Seek employment | 4% | 5% | 3% |
| Other | 3% | 3% | 2% |

[4] It should be noted that the percentages of A-Level students aspiring to go to university include those who wish to pursue a teaching career, but desire to do so after obtaining a first degree. This explains the apparent disparity between the numbers expressing a desire to pursue teaching (see Table 5) and those wishing to go to teacher training college.

**36.** In reports of preferred first and second career choices, teaching as a career was named as a first choice by 151 pupils (15%) and as a second choice by 147 pupils (17%). Thus, approximately one third of the whole sample of A-Level students were seriously considering teaching as a career option. Of these, 101 were female (67%) and 50 male (33%). Of the 147 pupils who said that teaching would be their second choice, 82 were female (56%) and 65 were male (44%).

**37.** The questionnaire included the following questions as to whether teaching fitted into their career plans and what kind of teaching has been or would be considered:

- have you ever considered a career in teaching?
- if you have considered teaching what kind did you consider?
- if you had to choose teaching, what kind would you consider?

Analysis of the data generated in response to these questions (Table 5) indicates that almost equal numbers of males (42%) and females (46%) say they have teaching as their first or second career choice. However a higher proportion of females (20%) than males (12%) indicated having a career in teaching as their first choice. Moreover, almost twice as many males as females report that they have never considered teaching as a career option (39% and 22% respectively).

Table 5: Are you considering a career in teaching? [5]
   *(A-Level students)*

| Response | All (n=1036) | Males (n=478) | Females (n=558) |
|---|---|---|---|
| Yes, that is my choice | 16% | 12% | 20% |
| Yes, but it's not my first choice | 28% | 30% | 26% |
| Yes, but I've changed my mind | 26% | 20% | 32% |
| No, never | 30% | 39% | 22% |

[5] Not all respondents completed every item in the questionnaire. In this and subsequent tables 'n' refers to the number of respondents in each category who completed the relevant section.

**38.** Table 6 is the first of a number of tables which illustrate the general gender-based attitudinal patterns which inform the focus of this study. This table refers to A-Level students who are considering teaching either as a first or second choice and elaborates the data presented in Table 5. It reveals that of the 42% of all males giving serious consideration to teaching as a career, there is a clear bias in favour of secondary teaching with more than half (53%) aspiring to working in a secondary school while only 22% are considering primary teaching. On the other hand, among females there is a tendency towards favouring primary teaching in their career considerations.

**Table 6: If you did consider teaching (first or second choice) what sector did you consider?**
*(A-Level students)*

| Sector Considered | All (n=532) | Males (n=218) | Females (n=314) |
|---|---|---|---|
| Secondary | 38% | 53% | 28% |
| Primary | 35% | 22% | 44% |
| Both | 23% | 21% | 25% |
| Other | 3% | 4% | 3% |

**39.** Those who have never considered teaching were asked what kind of teaching they would consider if they were 'forced' to choose (respondents were not given the option 'both'). Table 7 presents their responses in summary form and further illustrates the general male and female dispositions with regard to primary and secondary teaching. The pattern of responses is very similar to the pattern among those who are considering teaching, with males leaning heavily towards secondary teaching and females more inclined to favour primary teaching.

Table 7: If you had to choose teaching, what kind would you consider?
*(A-Level students not choosing teaching)*

| Sector of Choice | All (n=532) | Males (n=218) | Females (n=314) |
|---|---|---|---|
| Secondary | 42% | 51% | 35% |
| Primary | 36% | 23% | 47% |
| Don't know | 22% | 26% | 18% |

**40.** The responses of the total sample of sixth-formers as to the degree of certainty associated with their career choice are presented in Table 8. The table also includes an analysis of the responses of the sub-sample who answered the question, 'Have you ever considered becoming a teacher?' with 'Yes, I would like to be a teacher' or 'Yes, but teaching would not be my first choice', for the degree of certainty associated with their choice of teaching. The table presents an analysis of responses by teaching sector and additionally, for comparison, includes analysis of the responses of those not choosing teaching. Almost 75% of all respondents stated that they were 'very certain' or 'reasonably certain' about the career option they suggested, with females being marginally more certain than males. Thus, there is evidence that, at the sixth-form stage, respondents have reasonably clear career preferences and that these preferences vary in terms of the clarity or certainty with which they are held. Males and females aspiring to enter the teaching profession are not any more certain about their career choice than males and females not choosing teaching. No significant differences between males and females were found by tests of the significance of difference between means.

Table 8: Degree of certainty associated with choice of career (%)

*(A-Level students choosing teaching as a first or second choice and not choosing teaching)*

| Strength of Aspiration | All n=1036 | Favouring Sec. Teaching | | Favouring Prim. Teaching | | Not Choosing Teaching | |
|---|---|---|---|---|---|---|---|
| | | Males n=153 | Females n=121 | Males n=65 | Females n=193 | Males n=261 | Females n=243 |
| Very certain | 30% | 24% | 29% | 26% | 33% | 24% | 33% |
| Reasonably certain | 44% | 48% | 43% | 46% | 44% | 47% | 42% |
| Rather vague | 18% | 17% | 21% | 20% | 13% | 20% | 16% |
| Not sure at all | 8% | 11% | 7% | 8% | 9% | 8% | 9% |
| Sig. of difference between means | | ns | | ns | | ns | |

## Gender orientations in perceptions of teaching as a career

**41.** Sixth-formers were asked if they associated one or other gender with the career they planned to pursue (Table 9). Although the question produced almost a third 'don't know' responses, 42% of respondents saw their chosen career as one dominated by neither gender.

**Table 9: Perception of gender orientation associated with preferred career choice (%)**
   *(A-Level students)*

| Teaching is a career usually | All n=1036 | Favouring Sec. Teaching | | Favouring Prim. Teaching | | Not Choosing Teaching | |
|---|---|---|---|---|---|---|---|
| | | Males n=153 | Females n=121 | Males n=65 | Females n=193 | Males n=261 | Females n=243 |
| preferred by males | 19% | 28% | 15% | 17% | 7% | 29% | 19% |
| preferred by females | 10% | 1% | 14% | 14% | 22% | 1% | 10% |
| equally preferred | 42% | 48% | 48% | 30% | 44% | 35% | 44% |
| don't know | 29% | 24% | 24% | 39% | 27% | 35% | 27% |
| Sig. of difference between means | | ns | | ns | | ns | |

**42.** While only 1% of males choosing secondary teaching and 1% of males not choosing teaching see their preferred career as one considered mainly by females, 14% of males considering primary teaching are more likely to see this as a career chosen by females. At first sight, this hardly constitutes a substantial proportion and is actually less than the 17% of males considering primary teaching who see their career as a mainly male occupation. However, given the numerical dominance of females in primary teaching and the likelihood that sixth-form respondents are aware of this, the 39% of males considering primary teaching who claim not to know which sex prefers primary teaching (the highest 'don't know' response by any group) requires careful interpretation. It is reasonable to argue that a degree of gender-sensitivity is present among male respondents and therefore it is likely that this percentage (39%) includes males who are reticent to report that their chosen occupation is a female-dominated domain. It can also be noted from Table 9 that no significant within-group differences between males and females were found by tests of the difference between means (p>.05).

### Do males or females make the 'better' teachers?

**43.** In the focus group discussions, the issue of whether males or females make the 'better' teachers in general and in the primary and secondary sectors respectively, generated a great deal of comment and discussion:

| | |
|---|---|
| Male: | I think males are better at secondary school. |
| Facilitator: | Can you explain why? |
| Male: | Just, they are better teachers. But in primary school it is better for a girl. |
| | |
| Facilitator (to the girls): | Would you agree that males are better than females as teachers in secondary school? |
| Chorus of girls: | No. |
| Female 1: | I think they are equal. |
| Female 2: | It depends. |
| | |
| Female: | [If] men don't go into teaching, it's their own choice really. They can make as good a teacher as women do. |
| | |
| | I think it comes down to the individual person. There are some terrible male teachers out there and there are some terrible female teachers out there. I think each teacher has their own set of qualities that will stick out. A male seems to be the headmaster in a primary school possibly because they think there will be more discipline. |
| | |
| | There are different qualities for each one. Male teachers probably tend to get more respect. But then again female teachers probably have more compassion for the pupils and probably help them more, they are more of a mother figure. |

**44.** The questionnaire sought sixth-formers' views on this subject and responses are summarised in Tables 10 and 11. What is striking is the clear bias by all respondents, regardless of gender and whether or not they are considering teaching as a career, towards females as making the 'better' primary school teachers. Almost 60% of respondents felt that females are the 'better' teachers at primary level in contrast to only 2% who opted for males as making the 'better' teachers.

Table 10: Who makes 'better' primary teachers?
*(A-Level students)*

| Response | All | Favouring Sec. Teaching | | Favouring Prim. Teaching | | Not Choosing Teaching | |
|---|---|---|---|---|---|---|---|
| | | Males | Females | Males | Females | Males | Females |
| | n=1036 | n=153 | n=121 | n=65 | n=193 | n=261 | n=243 |
| males make 'better' teachers | 2% | 3% | 2% | 0% | 1% | 3% | 1% |
| female make 'better' teachers | 59% | 71% | 54% | 42% | 52% | 70% | 54% |
| Both make good teachers | 32% | 20% | 39% | 51% | 42% | 20% | 35% |
| No oppinion | 7% | 5% | 6% | 8% | 5% | 7% | 10% |
| Sig. of difference between means | | p<.001 | | p<.001 | | p<.001 | |

## Table 11: Who makes 'better' secondary teachers?
### (A-Level students)

| Response | All n=1036 | Favouring Sec. Teaching | | Favouring Prim. Teaching | | Not Choosing Teaching | |
|---|---|---|---|---|---|---|---|
| | | Males n=153 | Females n=121 | Males n=65 | Females n=193 | Males n=261 | Females n=243 |
| males make 'better' teachers | 22% | 36% | 12% | 34% | 12% | 35% | 1% |
| female make 'better' teachers | 6% | 3% | 4% | 5% | 5% | 6% | 6% |
| Both make good teachers | 62% | 53% | 76% | 54% | 77% | 48% | 71% |
| No oppinion | 10% | 9% | 8% | 8% | 6% | 11% | 12% |
| Sig. of difference between means | | p<.001 | | p<.001 | | p<.001 | |

**45.** No male respondent who is considering primary teaching suggested that males make 'better' primary teachers. Of all the groups, however, males considering primary teaching gave the highest rating to the equality of male and female primary teachers. While 70% of males not choosing teaching saw females as the 'better' primary teachers, this falls to 42% in the case of males considering primary teaching. This percentage of males considering primary teaching who see females as 'better' at the occupation of the career they themselves intend to pursue is still a substantial proportion of that group and illustrates the remarkably consistent notion among all respondents that females are somehow more appropriate than males in a primary school setting. It should be noted that this is consistent with the findings reported earlier from the sample of male primary teacher trainees (Paragraph 25) regarding their association of females with primary teaching. Additionally these findings suggest that sixth-formers' perspectives on teaching, like those of teacher trainees, are determined by whether the context is primary or secondary teaching. This suggests that stereotypes relating to 'teaching' differ markedly between the primary and secondary contexts.

**46.** With regard to who makes the 'better' primary teachers, the means for the responses of males and females considering primary teaching are not statistically significant (p>.05). However there are significant differences between male and female respondents in this respect among those considering secondary teaching and among those not considering teaching as a career (Table 10). As to who makes the 'better' secondary teachers, significant differences (p<.001) between male and female respondents occur in all three groups (Table 11). The strong bias towards females as the 'better' primary school teachers (59% of all sixth-form respondents) contrasts with the 6% of this sample who regard women as 'better' teachers at secondary level. Males are regarded more highly at secondary level with 22% of all respondents and 35% of males not considering teaching suggesting that men make 'better' secondary teachers. Perhaps predictably, males considering secondary teaching constitute the cohort most likely to see males as the 'better' secondary teachers (36%). Although small numbers of female respondents, whether considering teaching or not, see female teachers as 'better' than male teachers at secondary level, over 70% of females in all three groups in Table 11 ascribe equality to men and women as making good secondary teachers.

**47.** As was shown for primary teacher trainees (Paragraph 26), the general male bias towards females as the 'better' primary school teachers points to an association, in the perceptions of males, between women and primary school teaching. This association, combined with the gender-sensitivity of males indicated by the findings presented in Table 9, helps to illuminate the factors inherent in the relative lack of enthusiasm among male sixth-form students for choosing primary teaching as a career. The argument of Thomas (1984), reported in Paragraph 16, that, when career choices are being made, there is likely to be an interplay among a range of factors involving social, economic, circumstantial and individual variables, is relevant here. Although he did not make specific reference to the internalised images associated with particular careers (which operate often at a subconscious level, having been generated and subsequently internalised by individuals in the course of their everyday experience), it is reasonable to suggest that they are among the variables to which he refers. The findings above indicate that these internalised images and associations relate to the 'femaleness' of primary teaching and that they operate as a 'push' factor among males - for whom there is perhaps a socially-determined wish not to pursue a 'female' career.

## *Perceptions of teaching relative to other occupations*

**48.** To further examine the perceptions of teaching as an occupation among those making career choices, data were generated on how teaching is perceived relative to other occupations. The questionnaire presented sixth-form respondents with a list of ten careers which they were asked to rank in relation to a number of criteria. The ten careers were: Computer Programmer; Lawyer; Engineer; Journalist; Accountant; Doctor; Politician; Teacher; Electrician and Nurse. Respondents were asked to select the three careers from the list which they see as of most value to society, having the greatest potential for job satisfaction, having the highest status in the local community, requiring good communication skills, being most suited to females, and offering the greatest potential for a 'good' salary. Below are some responses from focus group discussions and a table showing how respondents ranked teaching in relation to these occupations (Table 12):

### ■ *Potential for job satisfaction*

Female respondent
(choosing primary teaching): I just like the idea of working with younger children and helping them along and helping them start out in life. I just like the idea of that.

Male respondent: Well my primary school teacher had a nervous breakdown. I remember that he was always sick. It is probably a very stressful job.

Male respondent: They seem to get a hard time now, the teachers. Here it's not too bad, but in Belfast, the harder areas, you might see a different side... You get no thanks for the work that you do.

### ■ *Status in local community*

Facilitator: Do you consider [teaching] a high status job?
Chorus of 'No'.

### ■ *Good communication skills as a requirement*

Female respondent: [To be a teacher] you can't sit there and be boring and you have to show you love the subject. There's nothing as bad as the teacher just sitting there with no expression. I think that to be a teacher you have to be outspoken and have expression. If you were really shy it would be hard for you to be a teacher.

## ■ *Suited to females*

| | |
|---|---|
| Male respondent: | I think if you tell someone you want to be a primary school teacher and you are man, they would take a look at you – |
| Female respondent: | that's really sexist! |
| Male respondent: | But it's a fact. |
| Male respondent: | ...With all the reports of paedophilia I would say that if I had children I would feel a lot less secure with a male teacher teaching my children than a female. |
| Male respondent: | I think women have a much better temperament than men and would be much more patient with children in general. |
| Facilitator (to the boys): | What do you think your friends would say if you said you were really considering teaching? |
| Male respondent 1: | Now that we are almost adult you would get a bit of slagging. |
| Facilitator: | Why would they do that? |
| Male respondent 2: | Nobody likes their teachers! My friends would not say anything; they would just want me to do whatever I wanted to do. |
| Facilitator: | Do you think their attitudes would differ between teaching in a primary school or a secondary school? |
| Male respondent 1: | Yes. It is more normal for men to teach in secondary schools... |
| Facilitator (to the girls): | What would your friends say if you said you were really considering teaching? |
| Female respondent: | Nothing. |

■ *Offer potential for a good salary*

| Facilitator: | Is there anything that would put you off teaching? |
| Male Respondent: | Probably the money. |
| | |
| Male respondent: | It's not entirely brilliant pay. It is not paid what it should be. |
| | |
| Female respondent | (choosing to be a teacher): I think it is badly paid but I think it is better to enjoy your job. You are going to have it for the rest of your life, so to me it's probably more important than the money. |

Table 12: Perception of Careers - Rank order by gender
   (*A-Level students*)

| Occupation | Value to society | | Potential for job satisfaction | | Status in the local community | | Requiring personal comm. skills | | Most suited to females | | Potential for good salary | |
|---|---|---|---|---|---|---|---|---|---|---|---|---|
| | M | F | M | F | M | F | M | F | M | F | M | F |
| Comp. Prog. | 8 | 9 | 7 | 8 | 9 | 8 | 8 | 10 | 10 | 10 | 5 | 5 |
| Lawyer | 5 | 4 | 3 | 3 | 1 | 1 | 2 | 2 | 5 | 5 | 1 | 1 |
| Engineer | 4 | 6 | 6 | 6 | 7 | 7 | 7 | 9 | 8 | 8 | 6 | 7 |
| Journalist | 7 | 7 | 4 | 5 | 6 | 4 | 4 | 3 | 3 | 3 | 7 | 6 |
| Accountant | 9 | 10 | 9 | 9 | 5 | 6 | 9 | 7 | 6 | 6 | 3 | 3 |
| Doctor | 1 | 1 | 1 | 1 | 2 | 2 | 5 | 4 | 4 | 4 | 2 | 2 |
| Politician | 6 | 5 | 8 | 7 | 3 | 3 | 3 | 5 | 7 | 7 | 4 | 4 |
| Teacher | 2 | 2 | 2 | 2 | 4 | 5 | 1 | 1 | 2 | 1 | 8 | 8 |
| Electrician | 10 | 8 | 10 | 10 | 10 | 10 | 10 | 8 | 9 | 9 | 9 | 9 |
| Nurse | 3 | 3 | 5 | 4 | 8 | 9 | 6 | 6 | 1 | 2 | 10 | 10 |

**49.** Males and females rank these professions, with regard to the six criteria, in much the same way. In the case of teaching, both males and females see it as the profession in this list which requires the best communication skills. Teaching is ranked second by both males and females with regard to its perceived value to society and its potential for job satisfaction. Neither gender ranks it quite so highly in terms of status and salary. Teachers are placed fifth, below lawyers, doctors, accountants and politicians, as far as status is concerned and are viewed as more highly paid than only two of the other professions, nurses and electricians. The career of teacher is very highly ranked among this list of professions as being 'suited to females', with females ranking it first and males ranking it second behind nursing. Both male and female respondents clearly associate teaching with women and this is indicative of the gendering of teaching referred to elsewhere in this report.

### Factors Influencing Choice of Career

**50.** Sixth-formers were presented with a list of factors which, on the basis of focus group discussion responses, might be taken into account when considering a choice of career. They were asked to rank these factors in order of importance (1 = most important and 7 = least important). The responses from the questionnaire data are presented in summary form in tables 13 to 15 below.

## Table 13: Factors Influencing Career Choice
### *(A-Level students)*

| Factor | All Males (n=471) | | | All Females (n=554) | | | Sig. |
|---|---|---|---|---|---|---|---|
| | Rank | Mean | SD | Rank | Mean | SD | |
| Perceived job satisfaction | 1 | 1.924 | 1.305 | 1 | 1.506 | 0.909 | *** |
| Salary | 2 | 2.207 | 1.204 | 2 | 2.578 | 1.123 | *** |
| Work mentally stimulating | 3 | 3.455 | 1.692 | 3 | 2.804 | 1.323 | *** |
| Status | 4 | 4.030 | 1.365 | 4 | 4.154 | 1.244 | *** |
| Good holidays | 5 | 4.491 | 1.361 | 5 | 4.791 | 1.182 | ns |
| Family approval | 6 | 5.334 | 1.121 | 6 | 5.390 | 1.010 | ns |
| Friends approval | 7 | 6.560 | 2.830 | 7 | 6.747 | 0.652 | *** |

*** = $p<.001$; ns = $p>.05$

51. From Table 13 it is clear that although the rank ordering of the factors by males and females is identical, there are highly significant differences between gender sample means for five of the seven factors ($p<.001$). These differences suggest that in the formation of career preferences, males attach significantly greater importance than do females, to extrinsic factors such as financial reward, the status perceived to be associated with their preferred occupation, and peer reactions to their choice of career. In turn, males report being significantly less concerned than females with intrinsic factors such as potential for job satisfaction and the prospect of the job being mentally stimulating. These gender-related differentials mirror the findings from the sample of teacher trainees (see Paragraph 19) and are also consistent with the outcomes of research reported in existing literature. For example, Ethington's (1988) findings were that males are sensitive to salaries and career prospects when choosing a career while females are more attracted to what they see as intrinsic rewards like job satisfaction. This said however, it is the case that females in the present study perceive the issue of salary to be an important consideration, having ranked it second out of the seven factors.

**52.** From Tables 14 and 15, which present the ranking of factors by those choosing primary teaching and secondary teaching respectively, it is clear that the findings reported above are sustained in each case. Although the rank ordering of factors by males and by females choosing primary teaching is identical, again there are highly significant differences between means for five of the seven factors (p<.001). Irrespective of which sector they aspire to work in, prospective female teachers attach greater weight to the perceived satisfaction of the job and its mentally stimulating nature. On the other hand, their male counterparts are significantly more concerned with salary, status and the opinions of their family, in the career decision they reach.

Table 14: Factors Influencing Career Choice among aspiring primary teachers
   *(A-Level students)*

| Factor | All Males (n=471) | | | All Females (n=554) | | | Sig. |
|---|---|---|---|---|---|---|---|
| | Rank | Mean | SD | Rank | Mean | SD | |
| Perceived job satisfaction | 1 | 1.984 | 1.533 | 1 | 1.473 | 0.820 | *** |
| Salary | 2 | 2.377 | 1.518 | 2 | 2.582 | 1.215 | *** |
| Work mentally stimulating | 3 | 3.803 | 1.806 | 3 | 2.892 | 1.327 | *** |
| Status | 4 | 4.082 | 1.370 | 4 | 4.141 | 1.217 | *** |
| Good holidays | 5 | 4.508 | 1.501 | 5 | 4.823 | 1.237 | ns |
| Family approval | 6 | 4.803 | 1.222 | 6 | 5.376 | 1.049 | ns |
| Friends approval | 7 | 6.599 | 2.042 | 7 | 6.694 | 0.762 | *** |

* = p<.05; ns = p>.05

## Table 15: Factors Influencing Career Choice among aspiring secondary teachers
### (A-Level students)

| Factor | Males Choosing Sec. (n=471) | | | Females Choosing Sec. (n=554) | | | Sig. |
|---|---|---|---|---|---|---|---|
| | Rank | Mean | SD | Rank | Mean | SD | |
| Perceived job satisfaction | 1 | 1.920 | 1.340 | 1 | 1.535 | 0.997 | *** |
| Salary | 2 | 2.332 | 1.129 | 2 | 2.737 | 1.168 | *** |
| Work mentally stimulating | 3 | 3.471 | 1.692 | 3 | 2.649 | 1.317 | *** |
| Status | 4 | 3.913 | 1.332 | 4 | 4.123 | 1.235 | *** |
| Good holidays | 5 | 4.442 | 1.440 | 5 | 4.763 | 1.131 | ns |
| Family approval | 6 | 4.879 | 1.225 | 6 | 5.345 | 1.040 | ns |
| Friends approval | 7 | 6.525 | 0.879 | 7 | 6.807 | 0.495 | *** |

*** = $p<.001$; ns = $p>.05$

**53.** Tables 14 and 15 illustrate that males considering primary teaching and males considering secondary teaching do not differ significantly in the weight they attach to factors which are important when choosing a career. Males choosing teaching therefore operate within the same value system when it comes to career choice, as do males not choosing teaching. They are guided by the same concerns and are much more concerned about the extrinsic aspects of being a teacher than are females. Likewise females considering both types of teaching display similar patterns of response to factors influencing choice as do females not considering teaching. It is therefore apparent that regardless of whether or not teaching is chosen as a career, there are gender-specific value systems within which males and females make career choices.

**54.** These patterns are reflected in, and are consistent with, the qualitative data from focus group discussions with sixth-form students and are illuminated by the analyses of data in respect of each of the factors potentially influencing career choice. The students were presented with attitudinal statements in the questionnaire, relating to a range of issues pertaining to teaching as a career and asked to indicate their responses using a five-point scale where 1=strongly agree and 5=strongly disagree. The means reported in Tables 16 to 20 below are derived from computations using these codes. For example, a mean between 1.000 and 3.000 indicates general agreement with the statement whereas a mean between 3.000 and 5.000 indicates general disagreement.

### ■ *Salary*

**55.**

| | |
|---|---|
| Facilitator: | What might influence you in choosing a career? |
| Respondent: | Money. A doctor has high status but he is also going to be well paid, he is going to get more than a street cleaner. So money is a factor in choosing a job, not necessarily for the status. |

| | |
|---|---|
| Respondent: | You want to be able to aim high. |
| Facilitator: | What kinds of jobs would be aiming high? |
| Respondent: | Ones that you know are well paid. |

As shown already, males are much more sensitive than females to the potential for pecuniary rewards when considering career options. From Table 16 it is apparent that there is no statistically significant difference between the responses of males and females not choosing teaching or between those of males and females choosing secondary teaching to the statement: 'teaching is a well paid job'. While these groups generally lean towards a view of teaching as not being well paid, what is striking is that the one group which perceives teaching to be a well paid job is males choosing primary teaching as a career. Females choosing primary teaching give much the same responses as the other groups. It is noteworthy that while females are more favourably inclined to the primary teaching profession than are males, they are less likely than males to see it as a well paid job.

Table 16: Perceptions of Teaching as a well paid job
(A-Level students)

| Group | n | Mean | SD | Sig. |
|---|---|---|---|---|
| Males not choosing teaching | 261 | 3.243 | 1.023 | ns |
| Females not choosing teaching | 243 | 3.385 | 0.966 | |
| Males Favouring Primary | 63 | 2.800 | 0.980 | * |
| Females Favouring Primary | 189 | 3.311 | 0.880 | |
| Males Favouring Secondary | 150 | 3.217 | 0.917 | ns |
| Females Favouring Secondary | 120 | 3.413 | 0.906 | |

\* = p<.05; ns = p>.05

## ■ *Job will be mentally stimulating*

56.

| Facilitator: | What influenced your choice of career?. |
|---|---|
| Male respondent: | Job satisfaction.... You want to be able to step back and say 'I have done such and such', you want to be able to be proud of what you are doing. |
| | |
| Male respondent: | I considered teaching before I decided to go for a career in computers. I looked at teachers; they just seemed to be doing the same thing every year... I just thought I couldn't cope with doing the same thing over and over. |

Respondents in all six cohorts see teaching as a mentally stimulating occupation to some extent, with females considering secondary teaching being the group most convinced of the challenging nature of the job. Males not choosing teaching are the group least likely to see teaching in this light. Males and females considering primary teaching report similar perceptions regarding teaching as a mentally stimulating occupation.

Table 17: Perception of teaching as an intellectually stimulating occupation
   *(A-Level students)*

| Group | n | Mean | SD | Sig. |
|---|---|---|---|---|
| Males not choosing teaching | 261 | 2.622 | 0.956 | *** |
| Females not choosing teaching | 243 | 2.315 | 0.890 | |
| Males Favouring Primary | 63 | 2.369 | 0.876 | ns |
| Females Favouring Primary | 189 | 2.326 | 0.908 | |
| Males Favouring Secondary | 150 | 2.549 | 1.006 | *** |
| Females Favouring Secondary | 120 | 2.267 | 0.932 | |

\*\*\*  = p<.001; ns = p>.05

## ■ *Status*

**57.**

Female respondent:  You don't want to be doing something that you are ashamed of. You want a job where people will look up to you and say: 'She is doing something worthwhile'. That is important.

Most individuals have perceptions of the status accorded to various professions and these can influence the desirability of a particular profession for those at the stage of making career choices. For example, an occupation perceived as having high status may be valued both in terms of the esteem associated with the job and in terms of the material benefits for individuals in the occupation. With regard to teaching as an occupation and the perceived status of teachers, all six groupings lean towards a belief that teachers are respected in their local community. No statistically significant differences are found between male and female perceptions of the status of teachers.

Table 18: Perception of the prestige associated with teaching
   (A-Level students)

| Group | n | Mean | SD | Sig. |
|---|---|---|---|---|
| Males not choosing teaching | 261 | 2.973 | 0.899 | ns |
| Females not choosing teaching | 243 | 2.275 | 0.852 | |
| Males Favouring Primary | 63 | 2.815 | 0.917 | ns |
| Females Favouring Primary | 189 | 2.782 | 0.813 | |
| Males Favouring Secondary | 150 | 2.895 | 0.882 | ns |
| Females Favouring Secondary | 120 | 2.735 | 0.844 | |

ns = p>.05

## ■ *Peer and Family Approval*

**58.**

Facilitator: Whose opinion would be most influential when thinking about career choice?

Male respondent: Probably your friends because you trust them more.

Male respondent: Your friends and peers. You don't want to do something where you will sell yourself short. If you do that then your friends will say you are a waste of space. But at the same time you don't want to aim too high. So your friends and your peers are there to say 'you are not aiming high enough, or you are aiming too high'. That's my experience.

Male respondent: My mother and father – they wouldn't push me anywhere, but they do want me to go to university and get a decent job in today's environment.

Female respondent: My parents are not pushing me in any particular direction; they said I can do what I want as long as I'm happy; but I think they have expectations that I will go to university.

Despite the frequent reference in focus group discussions to issues of peer and family approval with regard to career choice, the influence of friends and family was considered to be the least important of the factors which may be influential when considering a career. The questionnaire included two statements regarding potential reaction of peers to indication of a preference for teaching as a career. Tables 19 and 20 illustrate that for the sample of respondents in the study, males are much more concerned than females about a negative reaction from their peers if they say they are going to become teachers, irrespective of whether their preference is for the secondary or the primary sector. This would suggest that boys could possibly be dissuaded from choosing to become primary school teachers because of anticipated peer group reaction whereas females experience fewer concerns in this respect. Nevertheless, tests of the significance of the difference between the means reported in Table 19 show that in indicating a preference for becoming a primary teacher, male respondents considering primary teaching as a career are significantly less likely (p<.001) to predict a negative reaction from their peers than those males considering secondary teaching and males not choosing teaching. This might be because those males who have chosen primary teaching either have not experienced negative peer response or feel a need to be protective of their choice.

Table 19: Perception of potential for negative peer response to choice of primary teaching as a career
   *(A-Level students)*

| Group | n | Mean | SD | Sig. |
|---|---|---|---|---|
| Males not choosing teaching | 261 | 3.117 | 1.317 | ns |
| Females not choosing teaching | 243 | 4.451 | 0.848 | |
| Males Favouring Primary | 63 | 3.984 | 1.111 | *** |
| Females Favouring Primary | 189 | 4.538 | 0.784 | |
| Males Favouring Secondary | 150 | 3.085 | 0.916 | ns |
| Females Favouring Secondary | 120 | 3.248 | 0.946 | |

* = p<.001; ** = p<.01; ns = p>.05

**59.** Stating a preference for a career in secondary teaching also produces differences of opinion between male and females on the anticipated reaction of their peers (Table 20). Females considering secondary teaching are much less concerned about a negative reaction from their friends. What is interesting is that males considering teaching at both levels predict that their friends are less likely to be negative if they choose secondary teaching than if they choose primary teaching. This suggests that primary teaching is less acceptable than secondary teaching as a chosen career among teenage males and this must go some way to explaining the proportionally smaller number of males who opt for primary teaching compared to females who have no such pressures. While males regard teaching as a career which is reasonably well paid, carries a degree of prestige, and is mentally stimulating, a large proportion see it, particularly at the primary level, as a career which is somehow unacceptable.

**Table 20. Perception of potential for negative peer response to choice of secondary teaching as a career**
*(A-Level students)*

| Group | n | Mean | SD | Sig. |
|---|---|---|---|---|
| Males not choosing teaching | 261 | 3.243 | 1.020 | *** |
| Females not choosing teaching | 243 | 3.385 | 0.824 | |
| Males Favouring Primary | 63 | 2.800 | 0.921 | *** |
| Females Favouring Primary | 189 | 3.311 | 0.849 | |
| Males Favouring Secondary | 150 | 3.217 | 0.943 | |
| Females Favouring Secondary | 120 | 3.413 | 0.696 | |

\* = p<.001; \*\* = p<.01; ns = p>.05

## Section 6

**60.** In Northern Ireland, there has been a decrease in the percentage of males in the primary teaching workforce from 24% in 1987 to 20% in 1997 and this is reflective of the general trends in England and Wales. This 4% decrease is not uniform across Education and Library Board areas and both inter- and intra-Board variations are shown to exist.

**61.** During the last 20 years, there has been considerable volatility in the percentage of males in the recruitment to undergraduate primary teacher training courses in Northern Ireland. However, most recent figures show the proportion of males entering primary teacher training, while still low relative to the proportion of females, to be at the highest level since 1984. Although at face value this most recent trend is a healthy one, it does not guarantee that a male teacher presence will form a substantive part of every child's experience in the primary school stage of their education.

**62.** Factors influencing the choice of primary teaching as a career have not been studied in the context of Northern Ireland. Indeed gender-related issues regarding career decision-making generally, and with regard to teaching in particular, is under-represented in academic literature. This study sought to explicate the factors underlying recruitment to primary teaching with particular reference to gender.

**63.** Career decision-making among sixth-formers is shown to be a process in which males and females operate within different value systems. This is evidenced by the existence of highly statistically significant differences between males and females in the weight they attach to a range of aspects of a career. Rather than being black and white, these differences are subtle and contain nuances which require careful interpretation. This is emphasised, in particular, by findings regarding sixth-former attitudes towards primary teaching.

**64.** Male and female sixth-formers considering primary teaching as a career concur on the following:

- the status of teaching is not high relative to some other professions, but at the same time carries prestige
- career opportunity does not figure highly in choosing teaching as a career
- teaching is an intellectually stimulating occupation
- teaching performs a moral service to society
- primary teaching is associated with females
- their primary school teachers can be seen as positive role models in their choice of primary teaching as a career.

**65.** Male and female sixth-formers considering primary teaching as a career differ in a number of important respects:

- males are more likely than females to see primary teaching as a well-paid job
- males attach greater weight than do females to extrinsic factors in choosing primary teaching as a career
- males are more likely than females to experience negative reaction from peers about choosing primary teaching as a career.

**66.** More specifically, males considering or having chosen primary teaching as a career have the following perceptions of teaching as:

- a job in which their 'maleness' is necessary and of value
- a job suited to females, but not exclusively a woman's job
- a job in which a male presence might lead to a better balance in the gender composition of the profession
- a career choice which might be seen by their peers as inappropriate for males
- a job in which as males they may have to confront societal negativity about males working closely with young children
- primary teaching is a well-paid job.

**67.** Male sixth-formers not choosing primary teaching are likely to have been influenced by:

- the widening range of career opportunities available
- a preference for going to university and obtaining a subject-specific degree
- sensitivity regarding societal interpretation of males working with young children
- sensitivity about choosing a career in what is seen as a female-oriented domain
- concern about peer disparagement or disapproval
- negativity among their teachers towards teaching as a career.

**68.** Further research should be conducted to investigate how the quantity and quality of career information can be maximised and how the career advice process can be best matched to the needs of both male and females at the crucial stage of their career decision-making.

**69.** This study reveals the complexity of the nature of the career decision-making process and where teaching as a possible career choice is located within it. The findings both undermine and reinforce received wisdom regarding male and female perceptions of primary teaching. Notions of primary teaching are generated by a wide range of sources. The educational experiences of young people, teachers as role models, career advice received, the image of teaching in the media, attitudes among peers and relatives are internalised by both young women and men and account for their decisions about career choice. In exploring the importance and interaction of the many considerations that inform career choice, we can begin to account for the imbalance in the numbers of men and women entering the profession of primary teaching. The recommendations outlined at the start of this report suggest actions which will reduce this imbalance and encourage both young women and men to consider primary teaching as a career.

**Bibliography**

**Acknowledgements**

**Appendicies**

# BIBLIOGRAPHY

DfEE (1997) Statistics of Education, Teachers, England and Wales. London, HMSO

Ethington C. (1988) Women's selection of undergraduate fields of study: Direct and indirect influences. American Educational Research Journal. 25. 157-175

Evans H. (1993) 'Continuity and Change in All-Age Schools 1948-88' in D. Craig (ed.), Education in the West Indies: Development and Perspective. ISER Publications.

Ginzberg E. (1951) Occupational Choice, an Approach to a General Theory. New York, Columbia University Press.

Hill & Knowlton (1995) NOP Image of Teaching Survey (Report of research conducted for the Teacher Training Agency), TTA.

HMSO (1997) Teacher Recruitment: What can be done?', First Report of the Commons Education and Employment Select Committee, HC262-1.

Holland J. (1973) Making Vocational Choices: a Theory of Careers. Englewood Cliffs, NJ, Prentice-Hall.

Hutchinson G. and Johnston B. (1994) Teaching as a Career: Examining High School Students' Perspectives. Action in Teacher Education. Vol. 15. pp. 61-67.

Irish National Teachers' Organisation (1993) Equality of Opportunity in Educational Management. Dublin, Ronan Press.

Lortie D. C. (1975) School Teacher: A Sociological Study. Chicago, University of Chicago Press.

Newby et al (1995) 'The School Administrator as Multicultural Education Leader' in J. R. Hoyle and D. M. Estes (eds.), NCPEA: In a New Voice. pp. 184-193. Lancaster, PA.

Super et al (1963) Career Developments: a self-concept theory. Research Monograph Series No. 4 (New York, College Entrance Examination Board).

Thomas K. R. (1984) Occupational status and prestige. Vocational Guidance Quarterly. Vol. 33. pp. 70-75.

## ACKNOWLEDGEMENTS

The authors of this report wish to acknowledge with gratitude all those who made the research study possible:

The Equal Opportunities Commission for Northern Ireland for funding the study;

Ron Keegan and Joan McKiernan, EOCNI, for their general advice and helpful comments at all stages of the research;

The headteachers for access to their schools for the conducting of focus group discussions and administration of questionnaires;

The careers teachers for making the arrangements necessary for data collection and giving the research their enthusiastic support;

All those who took part in focus group discussions and completed questionnaires.

# APPENDICES

Questions used to stimulate and focus the discussion with groups of sixth-form students are listed below:

**1. What is your present career ambition?**

- *How long has student held this ambition?*
- *Did student choose A-Level subjects with a particular career in mind?*
- *Has student received careers advice at school/actively sought information about career options?*
- *Would student be disappointed/not care if ambition failed to materialise?*
- *Does career option require third level education? If yes, does student know entry requirement to third level institution?*

**2. What are your motivations for choice of future career?**

- *Probes: status; salary; prospects; requirements; family influence; peer influence; perceived job satisfaction; easy option; A-Level subjects constraining choice*

**3. Have you considered teaching as a career?**

- *If teaching has been considered, primary or secondary teaching or both?*
- *Does student expect to apply to a teacher training college next year?*
- *If teaching has not been considered can the student explain reasons why?*
- *Hypothetically if the student was to pursue teaching would he/she prefer primary or secondary teaching? Reasons?*

**4. What are your perceptions of the teaching profession?**

- *Probes: high/low status; high/low salary; job satisfaction; responsibility; holidays; easy/hard option; vocational; prospects; requires intellectual skills; requires management skills.*

**5. Reflecting on your own experience of teachers and teaching?**

- *Can the student think of a teacher he/she particularly admires/has been influenced by?*
- *If yes, male or female/primary or secondary teacher?*
- *What reason for admiration?*
- *Who are better teachers - males/females/same? Why?*
- *Secondary teaching most suited to male/female/same?*
- *Primary teaching most suited to male/female/same?*
- *What qualities make a good teacher?*
- *Are approaches to teaching by males and females different/same?*

## Career QUESTIONNAIRE !

1. Please indicate your gender. (Tick One)     Male                    Female
2. What school year are you in? (Tick One)     Lower sixth             Upper sixth
3. After you finish your "A" levels, what do you plan to do?
   Go to university          Go to teacher training college        Seek employment
                             Other  (Please specify)
4. What are your "A" level subjects?

   1 _____          2 _____
   3 _____          4 _____

5 - 11. Below is a list of factors which may influence choice of "A" level subjects. Please indicate
   your opinion of their importance by ranking them from 1 to 7 (1 = most important, 2 = next
   most important, etc. and 7 = least important).

                                              rank
   A. Being good at the subject            _____
   B. Friend(s) doing the subject          _____
   C. The subject is the best of a bad lot _____
   D. A future career in mind              _____
   E. The teacher of the subject           _____
   F. Interest in the subject              _____
   G. The subject is useful and practical  _____

   Other reasons for choice of "A" subjects are:

   _____

12. If your parent(s) are in employment, please indicate their occupation(s)
   Father_____ Mother_____

13. What career would you like to pursue in the future?

   _____

14. How certain are you about the career you would like to pursue?
   Very certain        Reasonably certain       Rather vague       Not sure at all

15. If you could not pursue this career, what would be your second choice?

_____

16. My preferred future career is one which is chosen mainly by: (Tick One)

Males            Females            Males and females equally            No opinion

17-23. BELOW IS A LIST OF FACTORS WHICH MIGHT BE IMPORTANT WHEN CONSIDERING A
CHOICE OF CAREER. PLEASE RANK THEM IN ORDER OF IMPORTANCE
(1= MOST IMPORTANT, 2 = NEXT MOST IMPORTANT, ETC. AND 7 = LEAST IMPORTANT)

|   | rank |
|---|------|
| A. Friends' approval | _____ |
| B. Salary | _____ |
| C. Perceived job satisfaction | _____ |
| D. Good holidays | _____ |
| E. Family approval | _____ |
| F. Status | _____ |
| G. Work will be mentally stimulating | _____ |

HERE IS A LIST OF TEN CAREERS AND PROFESSIONS.

| A. Computer programmer | B. Lawyer | C. Engineer |
| D. Journalist | E. Accountant | F. Doctor |
| G. Politician | H. Teacher | J. Electrician |
| K.  Nurse | | |

24. From the list A - K above, choose the three  careers which you feel are of most value to society.

    1 _____ 2 _____ 3 _____

25. From the list, choose the three careers which you feel offer the greatest potential for job
satisfaction.

    1 _____ 2 _____ 3 _____

26. From the list, choose the three careers which you feel are likely to have the highest status in
the local community.

    1 _____ 2 _____ 3 _____

27. From the list, choose the three careers which you feel most require good personal
communication skills.

    1 _____ 2 _____ 3 _____

28. From the list, choose the three careers which you feel are most suited to females.

1 ———— 2 ———— 3 ————

29. From the list, choose the three careers which you feel offer most potential for a good salary.

1 ———— 2 ———— 3 ————

30. Have you ever considered becoming a teacher? (Circle One)

A. Yes, I would like to be a teacher

B. Yes, but it would not be my first choice

C. Yes, I considered it in the past but have changed my mind

D. No, I have never considered a career in teaching

31. If you circled A, B, or C, what kind of teaching have you considered? (Circle One)

A. Secondary     B. Primary                    C. Both primary and secondary

D. Other (please specify) ————————————————————————————

32. If you had to choose to be a teacher, would you pick primary teaching or secondary teaching? (Circle One)

A. Secondary     B. Primary                    C. Do not know

If you circled A, or B, please give your reason(s) ————————————————————

33. Who do you think make better teachers? (Circle One)

A. Males          B. Females          C. Both the same          D. No opinion

34. Who do think make better primary school teachers? (Circle One)

A. Males          B. Females          C. Both the same          D. No opinion

35. Who do you think make better secondary school teachers? (Circle One)

A. Males          B. Females          C. Both the same          D. No opinion

1 = Strongly Agree   2 = Agree   3 = Neither agree nor disagree   4 = Disagree   5 = Strongly Disagree

36. Teaching is now more respected by the public than it used to be
   1        2        3        4        5
37. Most teachers would recommend teaching as a career
   1        2        3        4        5
38. Teaching is a well paid job
   1        2        3        4        5
39. It is easier to get into a teacher training college than university
   1        2        3        4        5
40. Teachers perform a service of moral value to society
   1        2        3        4        5
41. Teaching is an intellectually stimulating  occupation
   1        2        3        4        5
42. Most teachers I have known have a "calling" to teach
   1        2        3        4        5
43. To be a primary school teacher one must love children
   1        2        3        4        5
44. Teachers have a pleasant working environment
   1        2        3        4        5
45. I would consider teaching in the future but I want to go to university first
   1        2        3        4        5
46. Teaching is an easy  job
   1        2        3        4        5
47. Teachers have good career opportunities
   1        2        3        4        5
48. The community looks up to teachers
   1        2        3        4        5
49. Anyone can teach
   1        2        3        4        5
50. In primary school the role of a teacher is an extension of that of a mother
   1        2        3        4        5

51. Teaching is a demanding and exhausting job
> 1 2 3 4 5

52. Female teachers are more conscientious than male teachers
> 1 2 3 4 5

53. My primary school teachers seemed happy with teaching as a career
> 1 2 3 4 5

54. People become teachers because they can't think of another career
> 1 2 3 4 5

55. Children would be better off if all teachers in primary schools were male
> 1 2 3 4 5

56. More men than women become primary school teachers
> 1 2 3 4 5

57. More men than women become secondary school teachers
> 1 2 3 4 5

58. Primary teaching is a woman's job
> 1 2 3 4 5

59. If I told my friends I wanted to be a primary school teacher they would laugh at me
> 1 2 3 4 5

1 = Strongly Agree   2 = Agree   3 = Neither agree nor disagree   4 = Disagree   5 = Strongly Disagree

60. If I was to teach, I would only be interested in teaching PE
> 1 2 3 4 5

61. My primary school teachers were bad advertisements for teaching as a career
> 1 2 3 4 5

62. In primary school the role of a male teacher is an extension of that of a father
> 1 2 3 4 5

63. Female teachers are just as strict as male teachers
> 1 2 3 4 5

64. If there were no male teachers in primary schools, children would be disadvantaged
> 1 2 3 4 5

65. To be a primary school teacher it is essential to love young children
> 1 2 3 4 5

66. Male teachers get more respect from pupils than do female teachers
> 1 2 3 4 5

67. If I told my friends I wanted to be a secondary school teacher they would laugh at me

       1        2        3        4        5

68. It is inappropriate for males to teach young children

       1        2        3        4        5

69. Secondary teaching is a woman's job

       1        2        3        4        5

70. All primary school children should be taught by a man for at least one year

       1        2        3        4        5

71. Men are more suited to teaching in secondary schools than primary schools

       1        2        3        4        5

**And finally...**

*Have you any thoughts or ideas about why primary school teaching might not be attractive to males? Please give as much detail as you can.*

_____

_____

_____

_____

_____

_____

_____

THANK YOU FOR COMPLETING THIS QUESTIONNAIRE

1. Please indicate your gender. (Tick One)     Male        Female
2. What year are you in? (Tick One)        BEd 1     BEd 2     BEd 3     BEd 4     PGCE
3. If BEd, what is your specialist option? _____
4. When you complete your BEd/PGCE course, what do you plan to do?
   teach in N.I        teach elsewhere        don't know
   Other (Please specify)

5. What were your "A" level subjects? Please indicate your grade in each case in the brackets
   1 _____ ( )     3 _____ ( )
   2 _____ ( )     4 _____ ( )

6. If your parent(s) are in employment, please indicate their occupation(s)
   Father _____ Mother _____

| | rank |
|---|---|
| B. Salary | ___ |
| C. Perceived job satisfaction | ___ |
| D. Good holidays | ___ |
| E. Family approval | ___ |
| F. Status | ___ |
| G. Mentally stimulating work | ___ |
| H. Job security | ___ |
| I. Respectable job | ___ |
| J. Contribution to society | ___ |
| K. Promotion prospects | ___ |
| L. Imparting knowledge | ___ |
| M. Working with children | ___ |

A. Computer programmer          B. Lawyer          C. Engineer

D. Journalist                   E. Accountant      F. Doctor

G. Politician                   H. Teacher         J. Electrician

K. Nurse

8. From the list A - K above, choose the three careers which you feel are of most value to society.

    1       2       3

9. From the list, choose the three careers which you feel offer the greatest potential for job satisfaction.

    1       2       3

10. From the list, choose the three careers which you feel are likely to have the highest status in the local community.

    1       2       3

11. From the list, choose the three careers which you feel most require good personal communication skills.

    1       2       3

12. From the list, choose the three careers which you feel are most suited to females.

    1       2       3

13. From the list, choose the three careers which you feel are most suited to males.

    1       2       3

14. From the list, choose the three careers which you feel offer most potential for a good salary.

    1       2       3

15. Who do you think make better teachers? (Circle One)

    A.    Males    B. Females      C. Both the same        D. No opinion

16. Who do think make better primary school teachers? (Circle One)

    A. Males     B. Females      C. Both the same        D. No opinion

17. Who do you think make better secondary school teachers? (Circle One)

    A. Males     B. Females      C. Both the same        D. No opinion

1 = Strongly Agree   2 = Agree   3 = Neither agree nor disagree   4 = Disagree   5 = Strongly Disagree

18. Teaching is now more respected by the public than it used to be
   1    2       3       4       5

19. Most teachers would recommend teaching as a career
   1    2       3       4       5

20. Teaching is a well paid job
   1    2       3       4       5

21. It is easier to get into a teacher training college than university
   1    2       3       4       5

22. Teachers perform a service of moral value to society
   1    2       3       4       5

1 = Strongly Agree   2 = Agree   3 = Neither agree nor disagree   4 = Disagree   5 = Strongly Disagree

23. Teaching is an intellectually stimulating  occupation
   1    2       3       4       5

24. Most teachers I have known have a "calling" to teach
   1    2       3       4       5

25. To be a primary school teacher one must love children
   1    2       3       4       5

26. Teachers have a pleasant working environment
   1    2       3       4       5

27. Teaching is an easy job
   1    2       3       4       5

28. Teachers have good career opportunities
   1    2       3       4       5

29. The community looks up to teachers
   1    2       3       4       5

30. Anyone can teach
   1    2       3       4       5

31. In primary school the role of a teacher is an extension of that of a mother
   1    2       3       4       5

32. Teaching is a demanding and exhausting job

     1       2       3       4       5

33. Female teachers are more conscientious than male teachers

     1       2       3       4       5

34. My primary school teachers seemed happy with teaching as a career

     1       2       3       4       5

35. People often become teachers because they can't think of another career

     1       2       3       4       5

36. Children would be better off if all teachers in primary schools were male

     1       2       3       4       5

37. Primary teaching is a woman's job

     1       2       3       4       5

38. My primary school teachers were bad advertisements for teaching as a career

     1       2       3       4       5

39. In primary school the role of a male teacher is an extension of that of a father

     1       2       3       4       5

40. If there were no male teachers in primary schools, children would be disadvantaged

     1       2       3       4       5

41. Male teachers get more respect from pupils than do female teachers

     1       2       3       4       5

42. It is inappropriate for males to teach very young children

     1       2       3       4       5

43. All primary school children should be taught by a man for at least one year

     1       2       3       4       5

44. Men are more suited to teaching in secondary schools than primary schools

     1       2       3       4       5

45. I have always wanted to teach

     1       2       3       4       5

46. I chose teacher training because I was unsure of what else to do

     1       2       3       4       5

47. People are surprised when they hear that a man wants to become a primary teacher

     1       2       3       4       5

48. I was attracted to teaching by the prospect of being able to combine family life and career

     1       2       3       4       5

49. I would never want to teach in a secondary school

     1       2       3       4       5

50. Career opportunities are better in primary schools than in secondary schools

   1      2      3      4      5

51. I want to be a principal of a primary school some day

   1      2      3      4      5

52. There is a tradition of teaching in my family

   1      2      3      4      5

53. I have had experience of working with children in my spare time

   1      2      3      4      5

54. Fear of child abuse allegations was an issue for me when deciding to be a teacher

   1      2      3      4      5

55. In primary schools, career opportunities are better for men than for women

   1      2      3      4      5


Sometimes people describe primary school teaching as a 'woman's job'.
Why do you think they might do this?

_____

_____

_____

_____

_____

_____


Fewer men today are choosing primary teaching as a career. Why do you think this is so?

_____

_____

_____

_____

_____

_____

What do you think could be done to ensure that more men enter primary teacher training?

_____

_____

_____

_____

_____

_____

_____

THANK YOU FOR COMPLETING THIS QUESTIONNAIRE

Means reported below reflect the following coding:

1 = Strongly agree
2 = Agree
3 = Neither agree nor disagree
4 = Disagree
5 = Strongly disagree

Significance of the difference between means:

ns    no significant difference
*      $p<0.05$
**     $p<0.01$
***   $p<0.001$

| Quest Statement | Males not choosing teaching n=261 | Females not choosing teaching n=243 | Sig level | M Consid Primary n=63 | F Consid Primary n=189 | Sig level | M Consid Secondary n=150 | F Consid Secondary n=120 | Sig level |
|---|---|---|---|---|---|---|---|---|---|
| 36 | 3.096 | 2.948 | ** | 2.861 | 2.895 | ns | 3.091 | 2.942 | ns |
| 37 | 3.392 | 3.594 | ** | 2.861 | 2.895 | ns | 3.091 | 2.942 | ns |
| 38 | 3.243 | 3.385 | * | 2.800 | 3.311 | *** | 3.217 | 3.413 | ns |
| 39 | 3.082 | 3.799 | *** | 3.339 | 3.912 | *** | 3.039 | 3.636 | *** |
| 40 | 2.265 | 2.061 | *** | 2.123 | 2.041 | ns | 2.189 | 2.017 | ns |
| 41 | 2.622 | 2.315 | *** | 2.369 | 2.326 | ns | 2.549 | 2.267 | * |
| 42 | 2.438 | 2.066 | *** | 2.123 | 2.041 | ns | 2.189 | 2.017 | ns |
| 43 | 3.299 | 3.176 | * | 2.800 | 3.311 | *** | 3.217 | 3.413 | ns |
| 44 | 3.098 | 2.986 | ns | 2.923 | 2.912 | ns | 3.052 | 2.992 | ns |
| 45 | 3.340 | 3.149 | * | 2.956 | 3.001 | ns | 2.555 | 2.488 | ns |
| 46 | 3.727 | 4.264 | *** | 3.908 | 4.349 | *** | 3.692 | 4.233 | *** |
| 47 | 3.186 | 3.212 | ns | 2.908 | 3.146 | ns | 3.085 | 3.248 | ns |
| 48 | 2.973 | 2.775 | *** | 2.815 | 2.782 | ns | 2.895 | 2.735 | ns |
| 49 | 4.106 | 4.346 | *** | 4.262 | 4.368 | ns | 4.241 | 4.356 | ns |
| 50 | 2.897 | 2.803 | ns | 2.969 | 2.793 | ns | 2.882 | 2.876 | ns |
| 51 | 2.287 | 1.903 | *** | 2.277 | 1.854 | *** | 2.105 | 1.884 | ns |
| 52 | 3.122 | 3.205 | ns | 3.422 | 3.161 | ns | 3.111 | 3.158 | ns |
| 53 | 2.385 | 2.178 | *** | 2.339 | 2.131 | ns | 2.333 | 2.289 | * |
| 54 | 3.513 | 3.823 | *** | 3.908 | 4.349 | *** | 3.692 | 4.233 | *** |
| 55 | 4.159 | 4.428 | *** | 4.215 | 4.427 | ns | 4.183 | 4.525 | ** |
| 56 | 3.851 | 3.885 | ns | 3.877 | 3.917 | ns | 3.907 | 3.884 | ns |
| 57 | 2.831 | 3.257 | *** | 2.880 | 3.171 | ** | 2.830 | 3.266 | *** |
| 58 | 3.467 | 4.074 | *** | 4.123 | 4.088 | ns | 3.418 | 4.198 | *** |
| 59 | 3.117 | 4.451 | *** | 3.985 | 4.539 | *** | 2.993 | 4.421 | *** |
| 60 | 3.481 | 4.358 | *** | 3.708 | 4.406 | *** | 3.519 | 4.371 | *** |
| 61 | 3.734 | 4.070 | *** | 4.062 | 4.233 | ns | 3.730 | 3.983 | ** |
| 62 | 3.521 | 3.483 | ns | 3.554 | 3.503 | ns | 3.539 | 3.504 | ns |
| 63 | 2.515 | 2.113 | *** | 2.492 | 2.125 | * | 2.447 | 2.016 | *** |
| 64 | 2.397 | 2.615 | *** | 1.964 | 2.689 | *** | 2.414 | 2.542 | ns |
| 65 | 2.611 | 2.247 | *** | 2.400 | 2.266 | ns | 2.598 | 2.223 | ** |
| 66 | 2.776 | 3.323 | *** | 2.890 | 3.306 | ** | 2.669 | 3.272 | *** |
| 67 | 3.753 | 4.432 | *** | 4.108 | 4.391 | * | 3.934 | 4.529 | *** |
| 68 | 3.935 | 4.345 | *** | 4.477 | 4.224 | ** | 3.898 | 4.480 | *** |
| 69 | 4.170 | 4.409 | *** | 4.492 | 4.383 | ns | 4.250 | 4.488 | ** |
| 70 | 2.745 | 3.144 | *** | 2.539 | 3.166 | *** | 2.678 | 3.207 | *** |
| 71 | 2.701 | 3.384 | *** | 3.062 | 3.378 | ns | 2.565 | 3.455 | *** |

Means reported below reflect the
between following coding:

1 = Strongly agree
2 = Agree
3 = Neither agree nor disagree
4 = Disagree
5 = Strongly disagree

Significance of the difference
means:

| | |
|---|---|
| ns | no significant difference |
| * | p<0.05 |
| ** | p<0.01 |
| *** | p<0.001 |

| Questionnaire Attitude Statement | All Males n = 50 | All Females n = 284 | Sig of diff between means |
|---|---|---|---|
| 18 | 3.255 | 3.094 | ns |
| 19 | 3.706 | 3.853 | ns |
| 20 | 3.431 | 3.456 | ns |
| 21 | 4.431 | 4.537 | ns |
| 22 | 1.588 | 1.652 | ns |
| 23 | 1.843 | 1.924 | ns |
| 24 | 2.800 | 2.722 | ns |
| 25 | 2.784 | 2.052 | ns |
| 26 | 2.680 | 2.625 | ns |
| 27 | 4.420 | 4.632 | ns |
| 28 | 2.863 | 3.229 | *** |
| 29 | 2.627 | 2.878 | ns |
| 30 | 4.608 | 4.601 | ns |
| 31 | 3.325 | 2.858 | * |
| 32 | 1.529 | 1.497 | ns |
| 33 | 3.588 | 3.319 | ns |
| 34 | 2.353 | 2.367 | ns |
| 35 | 3.196 | 3.361 | ns |
| 36 | 4.216 | 4.472 | ns |
| 37 | 4.471 | 4.243 | * |
| 38 | 3.804 | 3.743 | ns |
| 39 | 3.216 | 3.462 | ns |
| 40 | 1.804 | 2.584 | *** |
| 41 | 2.941 | 3.337 | ** |
| 42 | 3.588 | 3.787 | ns |
| 43 | 2.314 | 2.760 | ** |
| 44 | 3.157 | 3.436 | ns |
| 45 | 2.137 | 1.937 | ns |
| 46 | 4.176 | 4.330 | ns |
| 47 | 2.745 | 3.014 | ns |
| 48 | 3.157 | 2.909 | ns |
| 49 | 3.843 | 3.389 | *** |
| 50 | 3.176 | 3.544 | ** |
| 51 | 2.412 | 2.955 | ** |
| 52 | 3.333 | 3.317 | ns |
| 53 | 1.961 | 1.711 | * |
| 54 | 3.412 | 3.632 | ns |
| 55 | 2.843 | 3.021 | ns |